MW01102091

Seven 7 Days
to
Confidence

Seven7Days
to
Confidence

Ros Taylor

with Dr. Sandra Scott
and Roy Leighton

LAUREL
GLEN

San Diego, California

Laurel Glen Publishing
An imprint of the Advantage Publishers Group
5880 Oberlin Drive, San Diego, CA 92121-4794
www.advantagebooksonline.com

ISBN 1-57145-776-3

Library of Congress Cataloging-in-Publication Data available upon request.

Project Editors: Elizabeth McNulty, Mana Monzavi

Design: Mana Monzavi

Printed in the United States by Von Hoffmann Graphics.

1 2 3 4 5   06 05 04 03 02

First published in the United Kingdom in 2000 by Vermilion,
an imprint of Ebury Press, Random House,
20 Vauxhall Bridge Road, London SW1V 2SA.

Contents

Acknowledgments

Rita Shamia must be thanked for her role in coordinating the input of all the consultants with Ros Taylor. Much midnight oil was burned by Liz Barker when assembling and typing the text. Of course, none of this would have been possible without the perspicacity of Janice Gabriel and Kudos Productions that the world and the BBC would be interested in changing the lives of 12 people.

And we should thank those 12 people who volunteered for the *Confidence Lab* project and allowed us to use their case studies for the book.

Foreword

When Kudos Productions first embarked on the making of the television series *Confidence Lab* for BBC2, we spoke to over 1,000 members of the public. Many of those who wrote and called us were ordinary people: managers, chefs, farmers, hairdressers, mothers, secretaries, board directors, unemployed people, and even police officers. They all represented a true cross section of the population and shared a fundamental problem: they lacked confidence, and this was preventing them from moving forward in their lives. What was also clear was that you would never know it by looking at them.

Of course, some people are very obviously shy, but we were amazed to discover just how many, who appeared outwardly confident and successful, found other areas of their lives more difficult to negotiate. It could be having the confidence to find a new partner, change their career, assert themselves at work, stand out at parties, or even sing somewhere other than their bathroom! Those chosen for *Confidence Lab* all reflected and struggled with very different, but common, confidence issues that affected them at home, at work, or in their relationships.

Often people know that they lack confidence but they have no idea what to do about it. The idea behind *Confidence Lab* was to introduce very practical skills to increase confidence to a group of six men and six women, during an intensive and challenging seven days of workshops at a country house. The most unique aspect of *Confidence Lab* was that we chose a combination of approaches from three leading facilitators: business psychologist Ros Taylor, psychiatrist Dr. Sandra Scott, and communications coach Roy Leighton. It was this eclectic and unusual approach that undoubtedly made *Confidence Lab* a success. The facilitators were able to monitor the progress of the "labbers," as they watched and analyzed their behavior on surveillance cameras—this was the "lab" element of the project.

This book offers you all the benefits of those seven days—without having to appear on national television. Here, Ros, Sandra, and Roy outline many of the exercises developed for the series, along with new ones specially adapted for you to do at home. They are simple and straightforward—and they work.

How do we know? After *Confidence Lab*, we followed our group back home as they went about their real lives and put what they had learned into practice. The changes they made were extraordinary and they now have a personalized "tool kit" of techniques with which to negotiate their lives successfully.

Janice Gabriel
Series Producer
Confidence Lab

The Authors

Seven Days to Confidence brings together three leading experts working in the area of building confidence and self-esteem. Ros Taylor, Dr. Sandra Scott, and Roy Leighton were key facilitators on BBC2's *Confidence Lab*, and they have combined forces again to bring you a practical tool kit of skills to help you gain confidence in just seven days.

Ros Taylor is a highly experienced business and management consultant and psychologist. She trained at Glasgow University and worked as a senior psychologist in Britain's National Health Service before moving into business in 1981. Ros developed "The Trans4mation Program" for her clients, in which she applies many of the principles here, along with new work that was developed specifically for *Seven Days to Confidence*. She has written a book outlining her work, entitled *Transform Yourself!* (Kogan Page, London, 2000), and her latest title is *Fast Track to the Top* (Kogan Page, London, 2002).

Dr. Sandra Scott is a psychiatrist at the Maudsley Hospital, South London. Her work challenges people's negative thoughts using the cognitive model and moves toward solution-focused goals. Sandra uses this approach in detailed case histories, and outlines a method that will help you challenge the way you think. Sandra recently appeared on the BBC2 television program *Predictions*, talking about happiness in the 21st century, and she is a columnist for the *Daily Mail*.

Roy Leighton is Head of Training at the London Academy of Music and Dramatic Arts, and he is also a management and communications trainer. His clients include Sotheby's and The Royal Albert Hall, and he is particularly involved with young people, working with Northamptonshire County Council on a long-term learning project. Roy brings a touch of drama to the mix, and many of his exercises use role-play and metaphor to illustrate his approach.

Introduction

We have designed this book to give you the skills to increase your confidence and apply the tools outlined here to your own life. Each chapter covers one day, but don't feel you have to do it all in one week. If you prefer, you can work through one chapter a week—it will still add up to seven days. However, you do need to read them in the order in which they are presented in the book.

The Seven-Day Confidence Plan

Here's what you can expect to achieve—and discover about yourself—in each chapter. On Days One and Two, the emphasis is on pinpointing why you want more confidence, from overcoming shyness to presenting to a roomful of delegates. Days Three to Six each focus on one key step of the Trans4mation Model of Change, developed by Ros Taylor: impact, thought, emotion, and action. The exciting thing about it is that, by improving the impact—or impression—you make, you'll start a whole new process of change. Transform negative thinking to positive thinking, communicate how you feel, and, best of all, take action to put the developments into practice—and experience confidence and success.

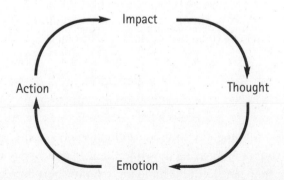

Day One
Getting Started

Getting started means defining confidence. This chapter shows how to explore personal issues of confidence and set goals for the future. Included are brief case histories of all the individuals who appeared in the *Confidence Lab*. You may recognize your own confidence issues in their stories.

Day Two
Self-awareness

In order to progress, we often need to look back, to reflect on where our beliefs and behavior have come from. The way our parents interact with the world will, in all probability, have affected the way we operate in the world. This is great news if they have fabulous social skills, and not so good if they don't! The good news, however, is that self-awareness promotes change.

Day Three
Impact

First impressions count. Here's how to create a memorable first impression, how to become sensitive to your own body language and that of others, and how to relax, so that you have everything you need to make a confident impact. Above all, you'll also discover what really inspires you—what motivates you from the moment you wake up.

Day Four
Thought

When we lack confidence, there are usually a number of unhelpful thoughts running around in our minds. Identifying these and discovering how they can hold us back is the focus of this chapter. Included are a number of case studies from Dr. Sandra Scott's work on the program, to show how you, too, can challenge the evidence of your thoughts and beliefs. Examining them in the cool light of day, and ditching them if they do not stand up to scrutiny, is positively liberating!

Day Five
Emotion

Day Five focuses on the ability to become emotionally intelligent. This means being aware of your emotions and those of others—both good and bad. Directly communicating how you feel and handling relationships are cornerstones of confidence. The way you reward, or "stroke," people acts as an emotional barometer, showing the warmth of your relationships and your ability to get close to those around you; complete the Stroking Patterns Exercise on page 87 to help you to assess the nature of your relations. Dealing with difficult people in an elegant way is also a major skill, so a four-step process to help you deal with your own difficult person is included along with sample scripts, so that you need never be tongue-tied again.

Day Six
Action

Action is the last part of the Trans4mation change process (see pages 110–131) and, without it, self-awareness would come to nothing. To increase your confidence, you must behave confidently. You can talk and emote all you like, but you need to act differently for the change to stick. The joy, then, is that other people change the way in which they behave toward you—when you show that you are confident. Department store salespeople take you seriously when you return goods, and colleagues look at you with different eyes when you present information in a new, compelling way at a meeting.

Day Seven
Staying Confident

In this final chapter, we explain how to keep the momentum of change going. It is always great to return from a workshop or finish reading a book on a real high. Yet this can fade if you don't keep reminding yourself of what needs to be done. The sad fact is that we forget all too easily what we have learned and can quickly become demotivated. Written reminders, supportive friends, goals and objectives—all this is at your disposal; all you need do is ask. Success breeds success. You really can build on your new-found confidence so that, with practice, you'll start to apply these skills naturally and, of course, confidently.

A Final Word

Changing takes time and effort. Buying this book is the first step in recognizing that you would like more confidence—you've made your first decision. But this in itself is not enough. You will need to become experimental, trying some of the suggestions to see if they work for you. Create your own Confidence Lab and try new ways of doing things. If you treat the whole process as an experiment, it helps you to distance yourself from the outcome and feel less fearful. And, of course, sometimes you've got to try new things a few times before you can feel comfortable with them. Think about when you learned to drive. Did you just jump behind the wheel and speed down the highway? You probably had a number of lessons before you felt confident enough to venture into heavy traffic.

If you saw the film *Groundhog Day*, you will remember that it took a number of reruns before the hero realized what he was doing wrong, changed the way he communicated, and finally got the girl. It takes three weeks to replace an old, lack-of-confidence habit with a different one, and at least another nine weeks to turn that new behavior into a habit—not long, really, if you've been shy for over twenty years. In Margaret's case, it took a major change in lifestyle for her to gain her confidence—but she did it.

Margaret's Money

Margaret was recently widowed and had no idea what to do with the rest of her life. All her friends told her that she needed a job but the thought terrified her. She had not worked for twenty-five years, since before her marriage. She decided to try raising funds for local charities. She felt there were no expectations for her to succeed but she would feel that she was making a difference. Well, she was fantastic at raising money. She discovered that she was extremely persuasive. No one could refuse her and, after a couple of years, she won the Fundraiser of the Year Award. She was completely astonished at her success, but said that she was so completely captivated by what she was doing that she forgot about her lack of self-confidence and found herself in situations that she would never have contemplated previously.

Enthusiasm can conquer fears. We just need to know what excites and motivates us!

Initially, trying new ways of behaving may not feel entirely comfortable. You will probably have occasional successes, more frequent failures, and gradual improvements as you progress. Be open-minded and experimental. Imagine that this is your own *Confidence Lab*, and that you are a scientist observing your own, and other people's, behavior. The journey will then be endlessly fascinating and, ultimately, successful for you.

The exercises in *Seven Days to Confidence* will be most effective if you practice them at every opportunity. You will be able to apply the skills outlined in this book to any situation, at home or work, with loved ones or colleagues, from asking for a pay raise at work to complaining in a restaurant. You will be able to chat with strangers easily and walk into a room with confidence. We have included case histories to help you.

Remember, if you write things down, it is 80 percent more likely that you will actually do them! And that's very much what this book is about—doing it.

At the end of each chapter we have given you a checklist, so you can monitor your progress. And, before that all-important date, meeting, speech, or pay review, you can always refer back to this book to remind yourself of the tools you'll need. At the end of the book, we have also included contact information for all the guest therapists who have appeared in *Confidence Lab*.

Some lucky people are born with confidence, but the good news is that confidence can be built and developed. This book will show you how.

DAY 1 ONE

Getting Started

Most people, if asked whether they want to increase their confidence, would probably say "yes." So what happened to the old virtue of humility and our reverence for someone with a shy, retiring nature? The reality is that, if you want success in whatever you undertake, or to feel comfortable in a variety of social settings, or to handle relationships effectively, then confidence is essential.

What is confidence?

At the beginning of Confidence Lab, our 12 guinea pigs had very definite ideas about confidence when they first met as a group. Are your ideas similar?

We show what confidence is on the next page, but it is worth mentioning what it definitely isn't. Confidence is not about arrogance—strutting, boastful, bragging behavior that is often a defense used by unconfident people to protect their profound insecurity. Confident people feel secure in the knowledge of their talents and so are relaxed and keen to listen and learn from others. The arrogant are self-oriented, keen to hear themselves talk, and are so worried that they are not good enough that they have to boast at every opportunity. Never mistake this posturing for true confidence.

CONFIDENCE IS. . .

√ Doing what you want to do, when and how you want to do it

√ Being relaxed, comfortable, and secure

√ Believing in yourself

√ Not believing someone else is always better

√ Doing as well as you can so that doors open in the future

√ Setting goals that are not too high so that you can achieve

√ Not having a huge gap when comparing yourself to others

√ Not compensating for being insecure by acting aggressively

√ Having the ability to act confident, even though you don't feel it

√ Having the self-esteem to fail and make mistakes

√ Being comfortable and not worrying what other people think

√ Having the guts to achieve what you want

Do you agree? Add your ideas here:

__ __ __ __ __ __ __ __ __ __ __ __ __ __ __ __ __ __

__ __ __ __ __ __ __ __ __ __ __ __ __ __ __ __ __ __

__ __ __ __ __ __ __ __ __ __ __ __ __ __ __ __ __ __

> If one advances confidently in the direction of his dreams, and endeavors to live the life which he has imagined, he will meet with a success unexpected in common hours.
> –Henry David Thoreau

True or False Confidence?

Aaron Beck, the world-famous father of cognitive psychology, still travels around the world, although he's in his late 70s. He teaches young psychologists the skills of his trade. He loves to meet people and he is genuinely interested to hear what others are doing. He loves being challenged, saying that it helps him give his best. When he meets you again, he always remembers your name, and where and when he first met you.

Another renowned psychologist, who is almost as famous as Aaron Beck, was hosting a question-and-answer session about his latest book. A member of the audience challenged him about a point he had made. Instantly defensive, he started a heated debate which culminated with him angrily saying, "When you are as famous as I am, and have made as much money as I have, then maybe you can comment on my work."

So how confident are you? Check the "yes" or "no" box in response to the statements in the following Confidence Checklist to discover which areas you need to tackle.

CONFIDENCE CHECKLIST

		Yes	No
1.	Do you feel comfortable talking to strangers for the first time?		
2.	Do you make a good first impression?		
3.	Can you enter a room full of strangers and feel positive?		
4.	Do you enjoy going to social events where you meet a range of new people?		
5.	Do you find it easy to make conversation with a wide variety of people?		
6.	Are you relaxed socially?		
7.	Are you a motivated person at work and at home?		
8.	Is life fun for you?		
9.	Do you have high self-esteem?		
10.	Do you think you have a positive attitude about yourself?		
11.	Do you tend to think positively about your future?		
12.	Do you focus on your successes rather than your failures?		
13.	When you encounter difficulties, do you problem-solve?		
14.	Are you generally positive about other people?		
15.	Do you reward and compliment those around you?		
16.	Do you handle difficult people skillfully?		
17.	Do you handle and express your emotions appropriately?		
18.	Do you cope with conflict and resolve it?		
19.	Can you speak in public with ease?		
20.	Are you successful at job interviews?		
21.	Do you put yourself forward for promotion?		
22.	Could you become a leader of a group, team, or company?		
23.	In the past, have you ever successfully changed any aspect of yourself—a bad habit, for example?		
24.	On a scale of 1 to 10, where do you think you are?		

1 (low)   (high) 10

Obviously, if you answered "yes" to 23 questions and rated yourself at 10 on question 24, then you're super-confident and probably won't be reading this book. However, the majority of you probably had a mixture of "yes" and "no" answers. Now is your chance to turn the negatives into positives. Note the questions to which you answered no. List them below and make them your goals for change.

GOALS FOR CHANGE

Begin each goal with, "I want to..." For example, instead of the negative: "I don't feel positive when I enter a room full of strangers," write "I want to feel positive when I enter a room full of strangers."

_____

_____

_____

_____

_____

_____

_____

_____

_____

_____

_____

You are, of course, not alone in wanting to change aspects of yourself to become more confident. The Confidence Labbers had a variety of problems they wanted to overcome. Here are some thumbnail sketches. You may see some of yourself in them.

Confidence Case Studies

Nigel, 34, is a chef who can't stand the heat outside the kitchen. He's moving up into management at an exclusive golf club, but, with his lack of qualifications, he's intimidated by the challenge.

Maria, 39, is a victim support coordinator who becomes the victim herself when under the spotlight. Outwardly she appears confident, but at work, when she has to address a 200-strong group, her composure totally collapses.

Paul, 27, is a women's soccer coach who can't score his personal goal. He can't assert himself, on the field or off, but mumbles from the sidelines and crumbles when approached by women.

Emily, 23, is an attractive, articulate young woman who prepares to go grocery shopping as if getting ready for a party. Unfortunately, Emily rarely gets to the party because she spends such a long time worrying about her looks.

Jo, 43, found out her marriage was over when she read in a tabloid newspaper that her vicar husband had run off with the church secretary. Socially, she's at sea, and her self-esteem is at rock-bottom. She needs to build a whole new social life.

Daniel, 38, is a former playboy restaurateur who used to holiday in Barbados, but now lives at home with his mother. He's bankrupt and he has never written a résumé. He's got no money and no idea who he is without the status that money brings.

Mark, 35, is a bricklayer who yearns to become a poet. He has great difficulty communicating with people and fears upsetting them, but he appears so unapproachable that others feel intimidated by him.

Karen, 35, is an aromatherapist. She's read all the self-help books and completed many personal development courses, but when it comes to putting what she knows into practice, she sabotages herself, putting obstacles in her way, and doubting her abilities. She finds it difficult to "sell" herself.

Jane, 27, is a saddle-maker who fears a public failure at the first stage of setting up a new saddlery business. Her business is ready, but her lack of confidence means she's not.

QUICK REMINDERS

√ Review your Confidence Checklist on page 8 on a regular basis, every two to three months, to monitor improvements.

√ Goals are flexible. Others will come to you as you go through this book. Keep adding to your list on page 10.

Tony, 38, has fantastic ideas that he either keeps to himself or expresses as confused ramblings to his bosses at work. He hides his light under a bushel and is always told he's too nice. The trouble is, he won't move up the corporate ladder if he isn't able to sell himself succinctly.

Linda, 36, is a large woman who hides behind her body. She tends to overcompensate by acting like a happy helper and hiding her real feelings. She wants to feel confident enough to be her real self.

John, 32, is a small man with a big issue—his height. John is a probation officer and deals daily with difficult people. He is conscious of his height at all times (5'5"), and his negative self-image stunts his efforts when approaching people socially and at work.

The process of assessment in itself can be sufficient to make a difference. One prospective candidate for *Confidence Lab*, Kathryn, made fast progress due to feedback from her family.

Kathryn's Turnabout

Kathryn was enthusiastic about do-it-yourself projects around the house, only to be derided by her husband and children. Her color schemes were very bright and clashed, but the overall effect was exuberant. The film crew interviewed her family and revealed to them that they were one source of Kathryn's lack of confidence. They were shamed into changing their attitude and, instead, became rather proud of her. Sadly for us, she improved so much that she had to be dismissed from the program!

All, or some, of these stories may be familiar to you. When reading the case studies, you may empathize with the Confidence Labbers' problems. Read on and complete your first Progress Diary to review what you've learned from Day One. As you work your way through each Day, look back to these early diaries. You'll see just how far you've come in less than one week.

PROGRESS DIARY

What I've learned from this chapter	How I intend to put this into practice
1.	
2.	
3.	
4.	

DAY TWO

SELF-AWARENESS

This book is about changing people, not rooms or gardens. And unlike walls and pathways, when people are changing, there is often a lot of pain and angst, as past hurts are addressed and futures are planned.

What makes us different from inanimate objects is our ability to reflect on our behavior and to change direction with the results. If you don't allow yourself this reflection, then the skills you learn will feel superficial—a quick fix rather than a long-term solution. So let's start a journey into the past and review what, and who, has influenced you throughout your life.

JOURNEY INTO THE PAST

Complete the following questionnaire.

1. What is your first memory as a child? _____
_____

2. Who did you enjoy being with? _____
_____

3. Who or what did you fear? _____
_____

4. Who undermined you and made you feel bad about yourself?
_____

5. Where are they now? _____
_____

6. Who motivated you to do more than you thought you could?

_____

7. Describe your best childhood experience. _ _ _ _ _ _ _ _ _ _

_____

8. Describe your most traumatic childhood experience. _ _ _ _ _ _

_____

9. When were you most carefree? _ _ _ _ _ _ _ _ _ _ _ _

_____

10. How did that feel? _ _ _ _ _ _ _ _ _ _ _ _ _ _

_____

11. On what occasion did you feel really good about yourself?

_____

12. When were your parents or close relatives most proud of you?

> It is never too late to be what you might have been.
> –George Eliot

_____

13. When did you last have an uproariously funny time? _ _ _ _ _ _

_____

14. When were you last completely relaxed? _ _ _ _ _ _ _ _ _ _

_____

15. Overall, are your memories positive or negative? _ _ _ _ _ _ _

_____

Look at your responses to the questionnaire. You will notice that, as you revisited your childhood, certain themes may have emerged. Did you have any upsetting experiences, for example, that continue to haunt you in adulthood? Now might be a good time to let them go or to forgive the perpetrators. Holding grievances eats away at you, and while the person you blame is probably oblivious, you are still holding these negative thoughts. This is a tremendous waste of your energy. Letting go of the past means you will have more positive energy with which you can move forward confidently.

Nigel's Story

When Nigel talked to Dr. Sandra Scott at *Confidence Lab*, he vividly remembered the day when his essay was derided by his teacher because of his poor handwriting. He felt stupid and that experience has remained with him into adulthood, sapping his confidence and making him doubt his abilities. He had to come to terms with his past to move on.

Also, consider your overall attitude to your childhood. If you think that all of it was unhappy, try to remember any happier moments between the more unhappy ones. You may have become so accustomed to looking at bad experiences that you have simply forgotten the good times.

How we perceive situations and events directly relates to how we think, feel, and behave. Explore this by trying the following exercise.

CASING THE JOINT

Imagine you are a burglar "casing" a house for rich pickings. In particular, you want to see the living room. Look at the photograph below for ten seconds, cover up the photograph, then answer the questions immediately, still in the guise of that burglar.

Questions

Respond to the following as quickly as you can.

1. What are the removable items in the room? List them.

2. Describe the curtains.

3. What piece of furniture would fetch the highest price?

4. How many plates could you see in the alcoves?

5. How would you escape if caught in the act of burglary?

6. Where is the radiator situated?

Any self-respecting burglar would have answered questions 1, 3, and 5 very easily. Questions 2, 4, and 6 may have been more of a challenge.

If you had been a real-estate agent or decorator, however, your results might have been reversed. In other words, your view of the world and what you do colors your thinking. You are blind to influences that do not fit your frame of reference. In the same way, having a negative view of the past can make you avoid situations and hold you back. So Nigel's negative experience with his teacher (see page 16) meant that, as an adult, he had constantly avoided promotion because he thought that he could not cope with writing reports. Happily, these beliefs have now been dispelled, and he is succeeding beyond his expectations.

To understand yourself even more, complete the PAC questionnaire below. It was originally designed by Eric Berne around 1960, but it has been updated by Ros Taylor at Plus Consulting. We will discuss it after you have finished and scored the answers. Stick with it. Some questions may seem beside the point, but it all makes sense eventually.

THE BACKPACK EXERCISE

Imagine that you are carrying a backpack. There's nothing in it at the moment, so it is very light. Now imagine that for each major experience in your life, a rock is dropped into your backpack. Walk around the room reciting those experiences, such as being born, starting school, being bullied, your first sexual experience, leaving home, your first major relationship. Your backpack is probably feeling quite heavy now. Really imagine how that feels.

Now take your imaginary backpack off and imagine how that feels.

The backpack containing all your experiences will always be there, but you don't need to carry it around every day of your life. Leave it at home once in a while.

THE PAC QUESTIONNAIRE

If you agree more than you disagree, write a plus (+) in the box.
If you disagree more than you agree, write a minus (-).

+ or -

1. Teenagers would be better off if they tried harder to understand the experience of older people.

2. I enjoy fast driving.

3. I am usually able to appear calm, even when I feel upset inside.

4. Too few people today are able to stand up for what they think is right and just.

5. Bossy people lack self-confidence, but they are not always aware of it.

6. I often get upset when people don't understand what I am saying.

7. In my opinion, good leaders aren't out to make themselves look good—they encourage people to give the best of themselves.

8. Television today is full of violence and sex.

9. I think it is perfectly natural to discuss sex, intimacy, and relationships openly.

10. Quitting bad habits, such as smoking or overeating, is extremely difficult for me.

11. The law should be more strictly enforced for those who break it.

12. Parents today let their children get away with too much.

13. I believe it is possible to be completely open and honest with others.

14. I feel that most of the major life decisions we make are based on our personal feelings and attitudes.

15. People are too easily influenced by others these days.

16. I enjoy long periods of silence.

17. As a child, I remember older people making me feel embarrassed.

18. Children need to be reprimanded more often for their own good.

19. The media today needs more censorship.

+ or −

20. Even with strangers, I seldom feel bored, impatient, or lonely.

21. I know that sometimes I ought to eat and drink less.

22. Knowing that others approve of me is important.

23. As a child, I was encouraged by my parents to learn and develop things for myself.

24. I do not like surprises or unexpected events.

25. Suicide cannot be justified under any circumstances.

26. I aim to involve myself in as much learning as possible, such as attending conferences and evening classes.

27. I know that I often talk too much.

28. Divorce should not be looked upon so lightly.

29. I do not get embarrassed easily.

30. I believe that many mistakes come from misreading a situation rather than carelessness.

31. I often feel uncomfortable when faced with awkward situations.

32. Compulsory military service would help a lot of young people today.

33. I have often had to change my strong views as a result of new information.

34. Humility is one of the greatest virtues.

35. I get easily annoyed with people who are meek and give in easily.

36. Experience is helpful, but always needs to be updated with new information.

37. Racially mixed marriages will always cause problems.

38. I want a happy medium between work and play.

39. I often have to remind myself that I don't make the rules; I just follow them.

40. It is impossible to change human nature.

41. There does not always have to be conflict between individuals and organizations.

42. I often get disillusioned and want to hide away.

+ or –

43. Capital punishment should be applicable in some instances.

44. People should practice their religion more than they do.

45. I believe in looking closely at the consequences before making a decision.

46. I often worry that people will disapprove of me.

47. I like to be in charge and in control of situations.

48. Even when socializing, I mix business with pleasure.

49. I prefer to be an employee rather than a boss.

50. I get bored easily.

51. Society would be a better place to live in if the laws were more strict.

52. I am not ashamed to cry in public.

53. I believe in speaking my mind when I think I am right.

54. I am jealous of people who can stop work and start a new lifestyle for themselves.

55. I find it difficult to trust people.

56. I am curious to work out new solutions to a situation.

57. I often put things off time and time again.

58. I am inquisitive, to the point of being challenging in relation to others.

59. People can lead self-directed and controlled lives.

60. Physical exercise promotes my well-being.

Compile your scores

Fill in your scores in the grid on the next page. Please note that the numbers in this grid do not run in sequence. Every positive answer you give scores 1; negative answers score 0. When you have inserted the points, add up the totals in the boxes and transfer them to the PAC Profile on page 22.

PAC QUESTIONNAIRE SCORES

Parent		Adult		Child	
1	☐	3	☐	6	☐
4	☐	7	☐	17	☐
5	☐	9	☐	24	☐
8	☐	13	☐	27	☐
11	☐	16	☐	31	☐
12	☐	20	☐	34	☐
15	☐	23	☐	42	☐
18	☐	26	☐	46	☐
19	☐	29	☐	54	☐
22	☐	30	☐	60	☐
25	☐	33	☐	Adapted child SUBTOTAL	☐
28	☐	36	☐		
Nurturing parent SUBTOTAL	☐	38	☐	2	☐
		41	☐	10	☐
32	☐	45	☐	14	☐
35	☐	48	☐	21	☐
37	☐	52	☐	39	☐
40	☐	56	☐	49	☐
43	☐	59	☐	57	☐
44	☐	**TOTAL ADULT** ☐		Natural child SUBTOTAL	☐
47	☐				
50	☐			**TOTAL CHILD** ☐	
51	☐				
53	☐				
55	☐				
58	☐				
Critical parent SUBTOTAL	☐				

TOTAL PARENT ☐

21

YOUR PAC PROFILE

Put a cross on the line for each of your three totals—parent, adult, and child. Do not worry about the different levels of scores—each scale is different. Now join the three crosses to create your profile.

	TOTAL PARENT score	TOTAL ADULT score	TOTAL CHILD score	
% 100	16	16	12	% 100
	15	15	11	
90				90
	14			
80	13	14	10	80
		13		
70	12		9	70
60		12		60
	11		8	
50				50
	10	11	7	
40				40
	9			
30		10		30
	8		6	
20		9	5	20
	7	8		
	6			
10				10
	5	7	4	
	4	6	3	
0	P	A	C	0

How to Interpret Your PAC Profile

The highest percentile score of your three scores indicates the "ego" state most used by you. If there is a difference of twenty or more on the percentile scale between the highest score and the second highest, this means that the highest scoring ego state is dominant for you. If there is less than 20 percent difference, then there is a likelihood that there is a switching back and forth between the two ego states; most people are not consciously aware of this.

What is an Ego State?

This diagram shows how Eric Berne, the father of a psychotherapy technique known as transactional analysis, envisaged what he called ego states.

> Skill and confidence are an unconquered army.
> –Geroge Herbert

Transactional analysis is a way of understanding behavior. It is based on the belief that we can learn from studying more closely the way our decisions and communications are based on our thoughts and feelings. Eric Berne proposed the concept that all experiences were laid down on a "tape" to be accessed when

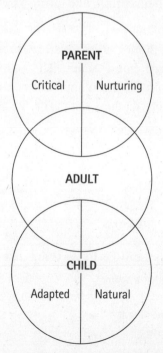

Parent, Adult, and Child Ego States

PARENT

Critical | Nurturing

ADULT

CHILD

Adapted | Natural

necessary. As soon as we pop out of the womb, this tape starts recording. The first people we meet are our parents, or parent substitutes, so they will feature hugely on our tapes. So let's look first at the parent ego, which is developed from our "parent" tape.

The Parent Ego

The basic information that we use comes from a lifetime of experience with your parents and teachers, particularly in early life. Remarks like "Sit up straight at the table," "Use your knife and fork, not your fingers," and "Bring it here, Mommy/Daddy will help you," will be on your parent tape and can be played back.

You can sometimes hear children scolding each other by saying, for example, "Don't touch that—Mommy says so." When we think, feel, talk and behave in the way we remember our parents did, then we are playing our parent tape. Often, the parent attitude shows in later life through what we say—for example, "Leave it to me," or "I will see to it."

The parent ego has two sides:

1. The critical, disciplining, and controlling parent.

2. The helpful, caring, and loving parent.

The controlling parent is the one who scolds when the children are late for dinner, and the caring parent is the one who is happy they arrived home safely. The parent ego is very strongly imprinted on the brain and works automatically, particularly if we are involved in any critical or evaluation process.

CRITICAL PARENT uses words and phrases like:

Words		Phrases
Right	Wrong	What will people say?
Good	Bad	That's the limit!
Never	Always	Why haven't you?
Sensible	Careless	You must never!

NURTURING PARENT says things like:

Oh dear, what a shame!	Don't be afraid.
Take care.	I'll help you.
Please remember to...	It won't take me long to...
Don't be late.	

The Adult Ego

All facts, logical experiences and common sense are recorded on your adult tape. The adult ego is the mature and deliberating part of you. Your actions and words, when this tape is played, are sensible and well-considered, as opposed to the almost automatic reactions of the parent ego. The adult ego collects information, evaluates it, works out probabilities, tackles and solves problems—all in a calm, collected way. As an adult, you concentrate on facts, not feelings and prejudices or emotional baggage from your past. The adult ego is independent of age. A child, too, can use common sense as a background for their actions.

ADULT ego asks questions and seeks facts, such as:

What is that?	Let's find out.
What do you think?	Let's experiment.
Why did that happen?	Let's define it.
What are the choices?	How can we handle it best?

> If you want your life to be a magnificent story, then begin by realizing that you are the author and everyday you have the opportunity to write a new page.
> *–Mark Houlahan*

The Child Ego

The child tape represents the child you once were. On it are recorded all your emotions, all your early experiences, together with your initial views of yourself and others. The child ego reacts emotionally with the feelings and instincts of childhood.

The child ego has two facets:

1. **The natural child,** who is primitive, impulsive, instinctive, undisciplined and demanding.

2. **The adapted child,** who carries the influence of a person's upbringing and learning does as it is told and may be manipulative. This gives rise to guilt, rebellion, obedience and compromise.

The child ego uses phrases like:

I like	You always try to	I will in a moment.
I won't	Let's play	If only
I must	Help me	If she can, so can I.
I feel	Wow!	It's mine.

Now that you know what parent, adult and child mean, let us look at your own profile and what it means.

YOUR PROFILE INTERPRETED

1.

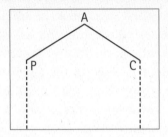

Behavior

This is a well-balanced profile with an equal measure of parent and child scores, but with the adult score gaining supremacy. You can remain cool in crisis and are therefore more likely to be confident.

2.

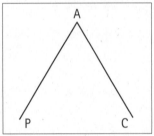

Behavior

You are very objective, cool and rational, but are you a little boring? The nurturing parent and natural child scores need to be higher if you are to become more emotionally articulate.

3.

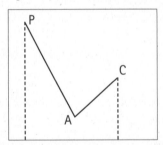

Behavior

You may tend to be authoritarian, either mothering people to death, or criticizing them. If this is your profile, examine the compilation of the "parent" score. Is it nurturing or critical? Either way, it needs to be reduced with more concentration on adult behaviors.

4.

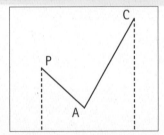

Behavior

If your score is high for the adapted child, then you could be too nice, polite, or ingratiating. If you're a high "natural child," then you are often the office wit but, sadly, often inappropriately so in serious situations.

5.

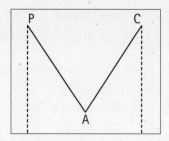

Behavior
This is an emotional profile fluctuating between demanding parent to ingratiating child. You are possibly argumentative, and rarely calm under pressure. Adult skills need to be encouraged.

6.

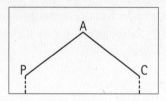

Behavior
Balanced, but low-scoring. This questionnaire may not be relevant to you if you have scored in this way.

7.

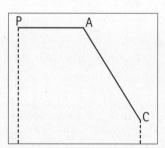

Behavior
You have good adult negotiating skills if you have this profile, but, when you are stressed, you may revert to telling rather than asking. You may be unaware when you are in parent or adult mode.

8.

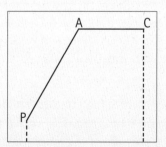

Behavior
This profile is the opposite to number seven. Again, you have adult skills, but you fluctuate between this mode and child mode. Look at your child subscore and work out whether you are adapted child or natural child. If adapted, you may be too polite in negotiating situations. If too natural, you may be inappropriately humorous on some occasions.

Personalizing Your Results

Adult Scores

The perfect profile for assertive, confident interactions can be seen in diagram 1. Here, the adult score is at least 20 percent higher than either the parent or child scores. That means you are cool, calm and able to negotiate. You handle difficult people well, never allowing yourself to get overemotional. If your adult score is higher than 16, and all your other scores are low, it would be suggested that you are too cool, or even cold. It is good to have a parent and a child score, especially a nurturing parent and fun-loving child. Life would be pretty dull if we were rational all the time!

Parent Scores

The chances are that you come across as rather authoritarian if your parent score is the highest and, if it is higher than, say, 15 points, you could be very authoritarian. Looking at your sub-scores, if you are more critical than nurturing parent, then you will probably have a tendency to blame those around you for your mistakes. This might be interesting if it weren't so irritating and demotivating for those around you. If your nurturing score is higher, then you will undoubtedly take on too much, as you like to help. But, in doing so, you tend to overstretch yourself.

Child Scores

The interpretation of high child scores depends on your sub-scores. A high adapted child score, higher than the other two, means that in conflict or negotiating situations you will opt for being polite. Sadly, in this world, some people take advantage of others' niceness to get their own way. Without losing your pleasant nature, you must learn the cool skills associated with the adult ego.

On the other hand, a high natural child score means that you are fun-loving and spontaneous. It's great to have a person like this around. The only down side might be that when discussions get tough, the high natural-child scorers tend to crack a joke to lighten the mood. Those of a more serious disposition will find that wildly inappropriate.

You might be in the position of having two high scores together, as seen in diagrams 7 and 8. This means that you use these ego states interchangeably, without knowing which one you are in or when. Here is an example.

A Heated Negotiation

Jim, who had been on a negotiating skills course, was discussing a fee structure with a supplier. The supplier was constantly trying to put the price up by adding on extras to the bill. Jim remained cool till the fourth time it happened. "Look, this is the way it is. Take it or leave it," he shouted, and then walked away. He knew he had blown it and put discussions back by months. His critical, authoritarian parent took over when he got stressed. Learning to relax and use additional skills cured him of that tendency.

These skills will be discussed during Day Five (see pages 81–109). So, if this is your failing, read carefully. To help you understand when you are in these various ego states, note the lists below of typical words, tones of voice, and the gestures associated with them. A lot of the time, we are oblivious about how we come across to others. And if we want to achieve confident interactions, then we need to gain self-awareness.

QUICK REMINDERS

√ Revisit your past and see what you're still carrying around that's no longer appropriate.
√ Do the Backpack Exercise on page 17, and leave your old baggage at home.
√ Remind yourself that perception is everything—if you look at old things anew, you might begin to feel differently about them.
√ Study your PAC profile.
√ Recognize which ego state is dominant in a certain situation. Is it appropriate?

WHAT'S YOUR EGO TYPE?

Check the words you respond to, to find out which ego states are typical of your behavior.

	Parent	Adult	Child
Words	Always	I believe	I feel
	Never	Who	Terrible
	Do like this	What	Help me
	Don't do that	When	Fantastic
	You must	Where	Wow!
	You ought to	How	I want that
	Never forget	Which	I cannot
	Remember the rules	Alternatively	Super
	What will people think?	Possibly	Stupid
	In my day, we used to	Often	Exciting
	Let me help you	My intention	
	Don't be afraid	Tell me more	
	You are wrong	Reasons for	
	Explain yourself	My reaction	
	Don't cry	What do you think	
	Be nice	Reality	
	Be quiet	Experience	
	Now listen	Let us find out	
		Here are the facts	
Voice	Critical	Clear	Teasing
	Bossy	Enquiry	Crying
	Encouraging	Relaxed	Playing
	Authoritarian	Factual	Shouting
	Comforting	Unemotional	Excited
	Stern	Harmonious	Amenable
	Sympathetic	Mid-pitch	Sensitive
	Protective	Affectionate	Submissive
Gestures	Pointed finger	Eye contact	Laughing
	Disapproving look	Nod of the head	Sitting hunched up
	Frown	Upright stance	Looking timid
	Stern expression	Relaxed	Crying
	Hug	Enquisitive look	Wide-eyed
	Pat on the back	Attentive expression	Grimacing
	Pat on the head	Thoughtful	Dancing around
	Arms crossed	Alert	Sulky
	Shaking the head	At ease	Head tilting
	Look over the top of glasses	Hands with palms open	Nervous

PROGRESS DIARY

What I've learned from this chapter	How I intend to put this into practice
1.	
2.	
3.	
4.	

DAY THREE

IMPACT

First impressions make a lasting impact. We might like to think that people should take their time to get to know the inner person before delivering a judgement. But it just does not work that way. So how can you know the way you come across to others when you first meet them? This self-awareness is difficult to achieve, since you can hardly ask every new person you meet, "What do you think about the way I walked into the room just now?" Well, you could, but not without being labeled slightly strange.

If you had a rating scale, with "confidence" at one end at 10 points, and "insecure" at the other end at 0, where would you land on that scale right now? If you tend toward the lower end of the scale, worry not. Help is at hand.

Here are a couple of examples of the difference a first impression can make:

John's Story

John lacks confidence to make friends because he feels insecure socially. When entering a bar or club in his hometown, he thinks that he should look tough to hide his feelings of vulnerability. He scowls, barely grunts, eyes directed at the floor, shoulders rigid as he marches to the bar. He looks neither to his right nor his left and, of course, people steer clear of him. John's body language creates the impression that you approach him at your peril.

On the other hand:

> Norman, in a similar bar in town, looks around as he enters to see who he knows or would like to join. He moves toward a group of people who are chatting and laughing. He goes toward them and asks what they do. They work at a nearby hospital and he is fascinated by their jobs. He nods with interest and asks more questions. Norman's body language is open and inviting, and they all end up going out for supper together and even agree to meet again the next week.

It takes 30 seconds to make an impression on someone but, when you walk into a room, people make an instantaneous judgement about you without your saying a word. Of course what you say is also important. Discover the impact you make by constructing your own 30-second commercial. In the space below, write a brief advertisement describing what talents, personal attributes, and skills you bring to your home or work life. Take no more than five minutes to prepare it and then exactly 30 seconds to read it through.

YOUR 30-SECOND COMMERCIAL

_____

_____

_____

_____

_____

_____

_____

_____

_____

Now perform your 30–second commercial in front of the mirror, or in front of a good friend.

Ask yourself the following questions:

- When talking through your commercial, was the language you used positive and about your strengths, or did some weaknesses sneak in?
- Did you use qualifying words like "fairly" good at, "quite" organized, or, I "think" people would say I was...?
- 30 seconds is not a long time, but did you use it well? Or had you just started when the 30 seconds were up?
- Did you use buzz words when you were making notes, or long sentences that took up too much time?
- Did you smile?

> Use what talent you possess: the woods would be very silent if no birds sang except those that sang best.
> –Henry Van Dyke

Now, perform your 30-second commercial again. This time, use positive statements and remember your body language. Above all, be confident.

This exercise isn't something you would choose to do every day. Boasting about your strengths is seen as, well, boasting! However, if you meet someone for the first time and they ask you what you do, do you say something positive? Is your answer crisp and concise, or do you ramble on in a slightly apologetic fashion?

You aren't saying you are the greatest person they have ever met—just good. If you believe it to be true, so will everyone else.

Remember, it takes 30 seconds or even less to make a first impression. Use your time wisely.

Body Language

How you look when you talk is of primary importance. Despite knowing how crucial body language is in terms of impact (see the chart below), we still focus on content too much of the time—what we say, not how we say it. Mehrabian's estimate in the chart is perhaps on the conservative side, as other researchers suggest the impact of body language is nearer 80 percent of communication. It is enough to know that it's important!

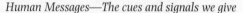

Human Messages—The cues and signals we give

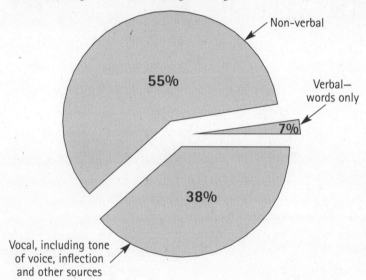

© Mehrabian 1969

In Allan Pease's book *Body Language*, he cites Professor Birtwhistell's estimate of ten to eleven minutes of conversation for the average person per day, with sentences lasting a mere average 2.5 seconds. The rest is nonverbal.

Take a few minutes to complete the stick figure exercise on the next page and compare your answers with those on page 37.

What are the stick figures saying to you?

So What Did You Think?

A. Thinking or pondering. This is internal, because the nose is in the air, shutting down eye contact.

B. This demonstrates a big emotion as it uses up a lot of space. It could be elation, or a gun in the back. We don't know—we need more information. After all, body language is only fifty-six to eighty percent of communication.

C. A relaxed or casual pose with hand on hip. If the foot is tapping, this could mean irritation.

D. Furtive or caught-in-the-act, the head is turned around, back hunched, knees bent.

E. Open gesture of welcoming or giving.

F. Despair or depression. Fetal position. Hands to face.

G. Anger, or certainly a powerful emotion. Needs to be checked out, as in B.

H. This is a coy, flirtatious, feminine gesture. Eye contact minimal, because the nose is slanted to the ground.

I. A don't-know, don't-care attitude.

J. Rejection. The nose is turned away, with the arms distancing.

> Do what you can, with what you have, where you are.
> —*Theodore Roosevelt*

There are no right or wrong answers, and the above are guidelines only. You would need a context and some movement to find out if you were correct. Here are further, nonverbal clues to the meaning of body language.

Body Language	What it means
Furrowed forehead, knitted brows	Thinking, perhaps not positively
Tapping foot and/or drumming fingers	Impatience, irritation, anger, agitation
Avoiding eye contact	Anger, concern, sexual attraction
Rapid, light breathing	Anxiety, fear, distress
Irregular breathing	Approaching important issues, controlling feelings
Deep, slow breathing	Suppressing strong feelings
Physical stroking of face, arm and neck	Comforting self or holding back the need for comforting
Touching face, neck	Uncomfortable or embarrassed
Scratching, pinching, severe pressing	Punishing self, reflecting self-criticism or holding back from provoking or punishing someone else
Controlled, low, quiet voice	Suppressing energy/interest, excitement
Fast, high voice	Excitement, tension, fear
Tightness/rigidity around jaw, neck, shoulders	Holding back anger, or upset
Clenching fists, tightness in arms	Holding back anger, or upset
Body leaning back, legs relaxed	Uninvolved, unconcerned
Arms tightly folded, legs tightly crossed	Defending, putting up barriers, resistance
Lounging extravagantly in chair	Detachment, cynicism, discounting
Hand covering mouth	Hiding, playing games, uncertain
Finger-jabbing	Critical, putting down, fencing with

Facial Expression

The face is likely to be the most expressive part of the body, telling us a great deal about the person, and yet we are often quite unaware of the expression we use ourselves. When we do look in the mirror it is usually with a fairly neutral expression, so we can remain unaware of the fact that our faces, which are open to people's interpretation all the time, may be telling a different story from our words and may be misinterpreted. Often the tense facial expression of the anxious person can be mistaken for quite different feelings like sadness, anger or disapproval.

Eye Contact

Often, the most attractive thing about people's faces is their eyes—not so much color, size, makeup or any other physical aspects, but the direction of their gaze. The extent of our looking at another person is determined by our relationship, proximity and the emotion being expressed. A direct stare for example, often indicates intensity of feeling of an amorous, hostile or fearful kind, while a deflected gaze is linked with shyness, casual superiority or downcast submissiveness. Messages of considerable importance can, therefore, be gleaned from observing changes in gaze behavior.

Observe two people engaged in conversation. The listener will watch the speaker closely, but will look away as soon as they take up the role of speaker. Disturbances of this standard procedure give us the shifty-eyed person who looks back for confirmation, and down in an attitude of submission too frequently.

Many of us handle eye contact as automatically as a very familiar dance routine, and we only become aware of its implications when there is some distortion. Newscasters, for example, by staring straight ahead while reading the teleprompter, can appear too familiar and even threatening. Thus, they try to break their gaze by looking down at their papers. When forced into a position of intimacy with strangers, such as a busy elevator, we all try to avoid eye contact by focusing on the floor or even struggling to face the door.

Those of you who lack confidence may find that your eyes plummet to the floor as you enter a room. You may think that everyone is looking at you, and that if you look away, you may cover your embarrassment. It's not only that this body language makes you appear uninterested and uninviting. More importantly, it says that you are not taking in what's going on around you.

Looking and Learning

In Nigeria, education professionals are training mothers and small children in direct eye contact. Traditionally, children were never allowed to look directly at their parents out of deference. However, it was discovered that Nigerian children were slower at learning from their environment than other nationalities because of this custom. The initial results of the training project are excellent, with children showing significant increases in their ability to learn.

To the same end, an ex-professor of psychology at a university encouraged his students to observe everything around them. "As you enter a room," he would advise, "gaze around at every face, always sit with your back to the wall and look at everything that happens as if it were a play unfolding in front of you. This way, life will be forever stimulating."

> **Wise words for the shy**
>
> When you engage with your surroundings, you realize no one is taking a blind bit of notice of you.

The additional benefits for the shy in all of this is that, when you engage with your surroundings, you realize no one is taking a blind bit of notice of you.

When giving a presentation, your gaze should be direct and prolonged eye contact should be used, especially when you're in listening mode. If talking to a group, you must gaze at each of its members as if you were talking to an individual.

Posture

This can tell us a good deal about a person's feelings. It is obvious that when we hold our heads up, straighten the spine and hold back our shoulders, we appear more confident. When frightened, humans tend to attempt to make themselves appear as small as posssible, with shoulders rounded, heads down and eyes avoiding contact. The other extreme is the brash, insensitive individual who sweeps into a room like a bull in a china shop.

> Posture becomes particularly important when we stand up to speak to a group or go to an interview. A manager who was very eager to be promoted, kept being turned down for positions for which he felt very qualified. He asked a development consultant for help, and it was only when they replayed a video of a practice interview that he discovered what the problem was.
>
> He thought that if he leaned back in a chair with his legs stretched out in front of him, he would look more relaxed. In fact, adopting that posture made him appear slightly bored and disinterested—not quite the impression he wanted to convey. Just by leaning forward and using some gestures to underline the points he was making, he looked eager and enthusiastic. Of course, he was offered the very next promotion he sought.

A confident posture is preferable to an apologetic one. Behave confidently, even as you enter a room or office. An erect posture helps you breathe deeply and reduces overall anxiety.

Gesture

The use and type of hand movements varies from culture to culture. In this country, we are often very suspicious of someone who uses a great deal of gesture, and yet this can serve very well to underline an idea or emotion that we are trying to express. Try giving directions to someone without hand movements, and you will realize what an aid they can be to communication. Other unconscious gestures, such as fiddling with a shirtcuff or bracelet when awaiting an interview, or tapping a foot when trying to appear fascinated by a conversation, may reveal emotions that we would rather conceal. Particular gestures, such as looking at a watch while someone is speaking, can be construed as insulting. Therefore, when we consciously wish to conceal our real feelings, we may try to suppress all physical evidence. Deceit, therefore, is often best achieved over the telephone, when only words and tone of voice can be attended to.

Gestures are good things. They underline important points and add emphasis to our speech. So keep your hands out of your pockets, and use open gestures as much as possible. Avoid folded arms or unnecessary fidgeting. The former looks closed and defensive, the latter very anxious.

Touch

The use of touch in a relaxed and unembarrassed way can be a great asset in many social situations. Most greetings involve some degree of physical contact and we have all reacted against the limp handshake, as we interpret this as someone's lack of interest or weak character.

Shaking hands when you meet and part from someone can help to build relationships. Try it and see how it works.

Distance

> Self-confidence is the first requisite for achieving great things.
> *–Samuel Johnson*

We all instinctively have a notion of our own space, and naturally we express this when conversing with other people. When someone moves closer than we wish, we perceive this as an invasion of our territory and withdraw from them in order to rectify the situation. In situations like the crowded elevator, we relinquish our space by adopting techniques to turn others into nonpersons, through reducing our movements, making our faces expressionless, and avoiding eye contact.

When you are in a meeting or making a presentation, make sure you are at a sufficient distance for easy scanning of your audience. Reorganize the room if you are ill at ease. When presenting with another person, it is good to sit by their side. This fosters feelings of cooperation. Small changes such as these can have big payoffs.

Own Your Own Space

When you have a good posture, all your internal organs are less squashed and can get on and perform in the way that nature intended. When we are squashed into ourselves, then our organs have to work much harder, which can deplete our energy or cause physical damage. Experiment with the Own Your Own Space exercise.

OWN YOUR OWN SPACE EXERCISE

1. Stand up (or sit) straight, and gently let your head flop forward onto your chest.

2. Relax your neck and feel the weight of your head gently stretching the spine (don't force it).

3. Now, imagine that your head is a balloon and is slowly floating upwards.

4. Open your mouth and, without forcing, slowly let your head flop backward.

5. Very gently, repeat this forward and backward movement several times.

6. Bring your head into an upright position and imagine that you have a piece of string attached to the crown of your head, which is being gently pulled. Don't raise your chin or thrust your head forward. You should be looking directly ahead now, and there should be no tension in your neck. Don't try too hard, as this can create neck tension.

7. Now imagine that your spine and head are aligned. There is a column of light radiating from the top of your head straight up into the sky. This is your space. Fill it. You cannot do this by merely imagining it. You have to feel that you deserve it. The more comfortable you are with deserving it, the more space you can then own.

8. How does it feel to be so huge? Walk around the room and enjoy the sensation of ownership.

Extend this confident attitude into other areas of your life. Go shopping, walk through the office. You will feel more confident and this, in turn, will have a positive impact on other people.

If you forget to own your space (and you will), then just envisage an imaginary puppeteer giving you a gentle pull up.

Relaxation

It's hard to make a good impact if you're nervous. Try these two short relaxation exercises, but not while driving, please.

THE POWER MINUTE

We all breath, and yet, believe it or not, the majority of us do it badly. The trouble is we don't notice this until a stressful situation occurs, such as before an important meeting or a new date.

1. Count the number of breaths you take in a minute (in and out equals one breath).

2. The average number of breaths you take is 10 to 12. More than this, and you are breathing too rapidly, and your breaths are too shallow. It's not so much that you are not taking in enough oxygen, but that you are not breathing out sufficient carbon dioxide. When we are tense, our breathing speeds up automatically so, by slowing it down, you also decrease the heart and pulse rate. Breathing out is the important part of the process, as it rids the lungs of stale air, stops us feeling dizzy, and makes muscles less cramped and sore.

3. Now, time your breathing again for one minute. This time, breath in and out more slowly while allowing yourself to slow down. This relaxed breathing is the POWER MINUTE, and it will energize you while focusing your mind on the business at hand.

THE FIVE-MINUTE NERVE-BUSTER

1. Sit on a chair with your right hand hanging by your side, and your left hand resting on your left thigh.

2. Close your eyes and slowly breathe in for a count of six, hold for a count of two, and breathe out for a count of four.

3. Breathe deeply from your diaphragm, concentrating on the blood flowing from your heart, down your right arm, then turning at your fingertips, going back up your arm and continuing around the body. Keep breathing slowly.

4. Focus on the fingertips of your right hand and become aware of a slight tingling in the tips. As you feel more relaxed, this tingling will get stronger.

5. After a couple of minutes, open your eyes.

You might feel that you can't confidently walk into a party or board meeting, complain in a restaurant, or ask for a pay raise, but perhaps you know a man—or woman—who can. Try the My Hero exercise to become more relaxed and confident.

My Hero: How to Take on the Characteristics of Your Favorite Person

- Think of the most confident person you know, living or dead, real or fictional.
- Write down the physical characteristics of your "hero" or "heroine."
- Write down the kinds of words and phrases they would use.
- Think of a scenario where you do not feel confident, or where you need to assert yourself, but find it difficult.
- Visualize the scenario, with you behaving the way you always have.
- Now repeat the scenario in your mind, this time dealing with the situation as your hero would.
- Does that create a different outcome?
- Practice this in the real world.
- You can use different heroes for different situations.

Nigel's Hero

Nigel's hero is Richard Branson, whom he perceives as calm yet inspiring, and someone for whom people just want to do things. Nigel's personal style is much more confrontational and, when he asks his staff to do tasks, they are less willing to cooperate with him because he uses a demanding tone and then gets upset! When he tried to ask for the same thing by using the attributes he associates with Richard, he used a more respectful tone, and requested that his staff help him to get his project in on time. The difference, of course, was astounding. His staff were far more willing to help out because they felt valued and respected.

Motivation

Motivation is linked to impact. If someone is motivated, they are automatically lively, energetic and enthusiastic. At work, motivation is essential. The Career Drivers Survey (from *Managing Your Own Career* by D. Francis) gives us great insight into which of the nine major "drivers" gets us up in the morning. Follow the instructions carefully, and then see how you fare.

Your Career Drivers

A word of warning before you complete the Career Drivers questionnaire section: sometimes, you will find yourself struggling to compare two items that appear equally relevant or completely irrelevant. But please persist. This technique forces you to weigh difficult choices, and the discipline will prove worthwhile.

There are no right or wrong answers—it all depends upon personal preferences, so be as honest and objective as you can. Work through the questionnaire quite quickly: ten minutes is usually long enough. First answers are best as they tend to be the most free of analysis or predicting how each will affect scoring the survey.

> Be thou the rainbow in the storms of life. The evening beam that smiles the clouds away, and tints tomorrow with prophetic ray.
> *—George Gordon Byron*

THE CAREER DRIVERS SURVEY

Instructions

Below are listed 34 pairs of reasons often given by people when they are asked about what they want and need from their career. You must evaluate the relative importance of the statements within each pair, and allocate three points—no more, no less. In other words, the possible distribution of points between the two items in the first pair, for example, would be as follows:

- choice one: A = 3 points   B = 0 points
- choice two: A = 2 points   B = 1 point
- choice three: A = 1 point   B = 2 points
- choice four: A = 0 points   B = 3 points

The letters given before each item are for the purposes of scoring and need not concern you at this stage. Just make sure that, when you have completed each pair, three points have been given each time.

1. A _____   I will only be satisfied with an unusually high standard of living.
   B _____   I wish to have considerable influence over other people.

2. C _____   I only feel satisfied if the output from my job has real value in itself.
   D _____   I want to be an expert in the things I do.

3. E _____   I want to use my creative abilities in my work.
   F _____   It is especially important to me that I work with people whom I like.

4. G _____   I would obtain particular satisfaction by being able to choose what I want freely.
   H _____   I want to make quite sure that I will be financially secure.

5. I _____   I enjoy feeling that people look up to me.
   A _____   Not to put too fine a point on it, I want to be wealthy.

6. B _____   I want a substantial leadership role.
   C _____   I do that which is meaningful to me, even though it may not gain tangible rewards.

7. D _____   I want to feel that I have gained a hard-won expertise.
   E _____   I want to create things that people associate with me alone.

8. F _____   I seek deep social relationships with other people in my work.
   G _____   I would get satisfaction from deciding how I spend my time.

9. A _____   I will not be content unless I have ample material possessions.
   D _____   I want to demonstrate to my own satisfaction that I really know my discipline.

10. C _____   My work is part of my search for meaning in life.
    E _____   I want the things that I produce to bear my name.

11. A _____   I seek to be able to afford anything I want.
    H _____   A job with long-term security really appeals to me.

12. B _____   I seek a role that gives me substantial influence over others.
    D _____   I would enjoy being a specialist in my field.

13. C _____ It is important to me that my work makes a positive contribution to the wider community.

    F _____ Close relationships with other people at work are important to me.

14. E _____ I want my own creativity to be extensively used.

    G _____ I would prefer to be my own master.

15. F _____ Close relationships with other people at work would give me special satisfaction.

    H _____ I want to look ahead in my life and feel confident that I will always be okay.

16. A _____ I want to be able to spend money easily.

    E _____ I want to be genuinely innovative in my work.

17. B _____ Frankly, I want to tell other people what to do.

    F _____ For me, being close to others is really the important thing.

18. C _____ I look upon my career as part of a search for greater meaning in life.

    G _____ I have found that I want to take full responsibility for my own decisions.

19. D _____ I would enjoy a reputation as a real specialist.

    H _____ I would only feel relaxed if I was in a secure career.

20. A _____ I desire the trappings of wealth.

    F _____ I want to get to know new people through my work.

21. B _____ I like to play roles which give me control over how others perform.

    G _____ It is important that I can choose for myself the tasks that I undertake.

22. C _____ I would devote myself to work if I believed that the output would be worthwhile in itself.

    H _____ I would take great comfort from knowing how I will stand on my retirement day.

23. F _____   Close relationships with people at work would make it difficult for me to make a career move.

    I _____   Being recognized as part of the "establishment" is important to me.

24. B _____   I would enjoy being in charge of people and resources.

    E _____   I want to create things that no one else has done before.

25. C _____   At the end of the day, I do what I believe is important, not that which simply promotes my career.

    I _____   I seek public recognition.

26. E _____   I want to do something distinctively different from others.

    H _____   I usually take the safe option.

27. B _____   I want other people to look to me for leadership.

    I _____   Social status is an important motivator for me.

28. A _____   A high standard of living attracts me.

    G _____   I wish to avoid being tightly controlled by a boss at work.

29. E _____   I want my products to have my own name on them.

    I _____   I seek formal recognition by others of my achievements.

30. B _____   I prefer to be in charge.

    H _____   I feel concerned when I cannot see a long way ahead in my career.

31. D _____   I would enjoy being a person who had valuable specialist knowledge.

    G _____   I would get satisfaction from not having to answer to other people.

32. G _____   I dislike being a cog in a large wheel.

    I _____   It would give me satisfaction to have a high-status job.

33. A _____   I am prepared to do most things for material reward.

    C _____   I see work as a means of enriching my personal development.

34. I _____ I want to have a prestigious position in any organization for which I work.

    H _____ A secure future attracts me every time.

35. F _____ When I have congenial social relationships, nothing else really matters.

    D _____ Being able to make an expert contribution would give me particular satisfaction.

36. I _____ I would enjoy the status symbols that come with senior positions.

    D _____ I aspire to achieve a high level of specialist competence.

Scoring The Career Drivers Survey

To score the survey, add all the points that you have given to each of the A, B, C, D, E, F, G, H, and I items. Write the totals in the boxes below and check that the grand total is 108.

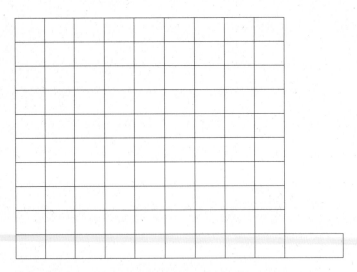

Copy these scores on to the Career Drivers Profile on the next page.

A	B	C	D	E	F	G	H	I		
+	+	+	+	+	+	+	+	+	=	108

YOUR CAREER DRIVERS PROFILE

Mark your scores on the chart below by circling the numbers you scored for each letter. Then join the circles to give a diagrammatic profile of your personal career drivers. When you have done this, read the next section to interpret your profile.

A	B	C	D	E	F	G	H	I
24	24	24	24	24	24	24	24	24
23	23	23	23	23	23	23	23	23
22	22	22	22	22	22	22	22	22
21	21	21	21	21	21	21	21	21
20	20	20	20	20	20	20	20	20
19	19	19	19	19	19	19	19	19
18	18	18	18	18	18	18	18	18
17	17	17	17	17	17	17	17	17
16	16	16	16	16	16	16	16	16
15	15	15	15	15	15	15	15	15
14	14	14	14	14	14	14	14	14
13	13	13	13	13	13	13	13	13
12	12	12	12	12	12	12	12	12
11	11	11	11	11	11	11	11	11
10	10	10	10	10	10	10	10	10
9	9	9	9	9	9	9	9	9
8	8	8	8	8	8	8	8	8
7	7	7	7	7	7	7	7	7
6	6	6	6	6	6	6	6	6
5	5	5	5	5	5	5	5	5
4	4	4	4	4	4	4	4	4
3	3	3	3	3	3	3	3	3
2	2	2	2	2	2	2	2	2
1	1	1	1	1	1	1	1	1
0	0	0	0	0	0	0	0	0
A	**B**	**C**	**D**	**E**	**F**	**G**	**H**	**I**

A   Material Rewards B   Power/Influence
C   Meaning D   Expertise
E   Creativity F   Affiliation
G   Autonomy H   Security
I   Status

WHAT DRIVES ME?

The nine career drivers

1. Material Rewards	Seeking possession, wealth and a high standard of living
2. Power/Influence	Seeking to be in control of people and resources
3. Search for Meaning	Seeking to do things that are believed to be valuable for their own sake
4. Expertise	Seeking a high level of accomplishment in a specialized field
5. Creativity	Seeking to innovate and to be identified with original output
6. Affiliation	Seeking nourishing relationships with others at work
7. Autonomy	Seeking to be independent and able to make key decisions for oneself
8. Security	Seeking a solid and predictable future
9. Status	Seeking to be recognized and admired

Remember to check that your total score is 108. Now, look at your profile and circle your top two or three highest scores. These are your main drivers, the sources of energy and direction that shape your life. If we are unaware of these career drivers, the danger is that we seek jobs or promoted positions because it is the next step, or we think that everyone expects it of us. If a job does not satisfy our major drivers we become dispirited, apathetic, even depressed—certainly the opposite of motivated.

Here is a list of things to look out for and ways to interrogate your scores. The most important question to ask yourself is, "Does my current position satisfy all of my main drivers?" If not, then you must consider changing your role immediately or as soon as is humanly possible. I know this is not as easy as it sounds. Mortgages and rents must be paid. However, there are often areas within jobs that you could volunteer for, or possibly delegate the areas of your job that you dislike to someone who would be motivated by them (give Career Drivers to everyone in your department or team). You can then concentrate on the more satisfying elements. You'll be happier and more confident if you are in control of your career.

> What changes could you make
> as result of this survey?

_____

_____

_____

_____

_____

_____

_____

_____

_____

_____

_____

> I am not afraid of
> storms, for I am
> learning how to
> sail my ship.
> –*Louisa May Alcott*

Alternatively, keep your resumé up-to-date and send it to some agencies or head hunters. It is always good to know your value in the market place, and this is a strategy used by fast-track managers to negotiate their way to the top. You do not have to leave your job; it just gives you the increased confidence to negotiate. On the other hand, this questionnaire may have confirmed your desire for new challenges. If so, then you can use your new knowledge of your drivers to interview the interviewer.

For example, those with a high B score—for power and influence—must ask who they will be reporting to, and if they will be given a free hand to carry out any improvements. High *meaning* scorers must ask about their level of involvement in decision-making, how they will know what is going on and where their job fits into the overall picture. Those of you who have a drive to be experts should inquire about the availability of training and coaching before ever considering a position, and so on.

Your top drivers will change over time. For example, one of my former colleagues in a large organization was eager to set up her own practice. Her highest scores by far were power and influence, and autonomy. This pattern, by the way, is predictive of entrepreneurial zeal. It may be coupled with a high money score but that is less predictive than the other two. Plan to do your own thing if this pattern is yours.

As soon as she had set up her own company with another specialist in her field, her drivers changed. Creativity became higher, as she wanted to do things differently, and affiliation increased, as she sought to surround herself with like-minded people.

Now her creativity score is still high as she constantly strives for new ways to coach and train, but a higher money score has crept in which was never there before, and that surprised her. This probably comes from a desire to achieve financial reward after constantly reinvesting in the company for years.

Look out for conflict between your scores. If you have a high autonomy and security score, then it could be that you are sticking with the wrong job because it is steady. Or, you are working for a charity and have a high money score—certainly the wrong place to be!

Another motivation generality comes from learning theory. In laboratory conditions, a wide range of animals have changed their behavior in order to gain reward.

As students, we all read about experiments with pigeons that learn to turn cartwheels when successive approximations to a cartwheel are rewarded with pigeon food. Psychologists might have electrocuted, spoken sternly to or beaten them to a pulp to make them learn, but reward worked best.

Humans are not dissimilar. During a recent research project into reward, it was discovered that for students to maintain a good performance, tutors had to reward them eight times as much as they criticized. And, to improve the students' performance incrementally, tutors had to reward them eight times as much as they criticized. This emphasizes the profound effect reward can have. Follow these rules to make yourself even more rewarding.

Rules for Reward

Intermittent

Rewards are most rewarding when they are intermittent, not predictable or institutionalized, like pay raises or bonuses. A thank you, a card, a box of chocolates on completion of an assignment are much more compelling. It's like gambling. If you were rewarded with a win every time you bet on something, there would be no excitement and, of course, no addiction.

Specific

Rewards should be "for" something well done or something that you would like to happen again. To be truly reinforcing, you should outline the specific behavior you admire, such as working late or going that extra mile, rather than just being nice, which is hard to repeat if you don't know exactly what you did to be nice.

Contingent

A thank you of any sort is more powerful if it is contingent on or given immediately after an event rather than a week later, at the end of the month, or at the end of the year. We associate good feelings that accompany the reward with the action that led to it and are more than likely to perform that way again. A managing director I work with, Iain Kennedy, phones me as soon as I have completed a training course for his staff to give me any positive feedback he has received. His feedback makes me want to work harder, longer, and more effectively to achieve that reward.

Consistent

If you reward one person for going that extra mile, you must notice and celebrate other extra miles. Unfairness and inconsistency ruin the entire process and lead to accusations of favoritism.

Relevant

Tap into your knowledge of the career-drivers of your friends, family or colleagues to choose a reward that is relevant and motivational. Take note of this cautionary tale of the managing director when trying to decide what will motivate others. A shipping company had gone through tough times during the recession but had recovered through the good services of the staff, who had put in extra hours and taken pay cuts. The managing director had dreamed of rewarding the entire workforce and their families with a Christmas cruise to celebrate the turnaround. But, as he jauntily put up the poster advertising the event, the workforce went on strike. I'm sure you can guess the reason. They would have preferred a less expensive party instead, and some money to buy gifts for their children, who had been deprived of luxuries during the recession.

Genuine

Flattery for the purpose of ingratiation or achievement can be easily spotted (especially in the tone of voice and body language). Rewards and compliments must be genuinely felt and sincerely praised.

THE TRAIN EXERCISE

You don't need to be an artist to do this exercise. Use the space provided, or just find a large sheet of paper and some bright marker pens. Do the following:

1. Draw hills
2. Draw a track
3. Draw an engine
4. Draw carriages
5. Place all the significant people in your life on the train
6. Draw and name them individually on the following page.

YOUR TRAIN EXERCISE

Now ask yourself a few questions:

- Who's on your train? Why have you chosen them? Where are they placed and why?
- Who is not on the train that should be? Are all your friends there, and is work represented?
- Where are you? If you're not driving your train, where are you? Why aren't you driving your train?

This exercise is really useful to pinpoint where you are in your life and whether you are in control of where it's going.

Write down what you have learned from this exercise.

What actions might you take, based on this exercise?

Jo's Story

In Jo's train exercise, she crammed all her friends and family into one carriage, leaving herself on top of the carriage, exposed to the elements and without a driver! She was so busy looking after everyone else, there was no room for her. She realized she needed to put herself first, so that she was driving her own train and in charge of her life.

PROGRESS DIARY

What I've learned from this chapter	How I intend to put this into practice
1.	
2.	
3.	
4.	

DAY 4 FOUR

THOUGHT

Thoughts are in our heads all the time—so much so, that they seem automatic, occurring as if by reflex. Often we are so used to them that we believe they are part of our genetics. This is, of course, untrue; we are totally in charge of what goes on in our minds.

To tap into your thinking style, complete the exercise on the following page, being as honest as possible.

When you have filled in all the spaces, judge whether your words, phrases or traits are positive or negative for all of the sections, and place a plus or minus sign as you see fit.

Reflect on the following questions:
- Did you have more positives than negatives overall?
- Did more negatives cluster in one section than in the other two?
- If you do have some negatives, why did you not consider a list of fifteen positives? And if you did consider it, what stopped you?

This exercise is about self-esteem, which researchers describe as being about a combination of worth and competence. If you have selected fifteen positive statements to describe yourself, then congratulations. If you have a peppering of negatives, then you must ask yourself whether these thoughts truly describe you now, or if you have progressed in competence and value beyond the adjectives you chose to use.

THE LABELING EXERCISE

Make a list of five words, phrases or traits that describe you best:

1. As you see yourself.
2. The view of a superior at work.
3. The view of a relative or partner.

Give yourself about five minutes to complete this exercise. Do not deliberate too long, as first thoughts are best.

(1) As you see yourself

I am _____

I am _____

I am _____

I am _____

I am _____

(2) The view of a superior at work

I am _____

I am _____

I am _____

I am _____

I am _____

(3) The view of a relative or partner

I am _____

I am _____

I am _____

I am _____

I am _____

We get so used to calling ourselves "shy," for example, that it never occurs to us to challenge this even after we have given that nerve-racking speech to the board of directors and then went on to celebrate at a party afterward. To maintain the thought, we might even say that it was easy because it was work. With strangers, it would have been more difficult. Although this might be absolutely true, you could, however, have said, "I conquered shyness at work—now all I have to do is tackle strangers."

Take your labeling exercise list to a good friend and ask them to go through it with you. Ask them the question, "Is the image I have of myself the image that others have of me?" You must be prepared to listen. Allow time to talk and ask questions to encourage their honest feedback. Refrain from seeking to explain or justify what you have written.

Also, ask yourself if you have negatives in sections two and three, i.e., a view of a superior at work or relative/partner. Why are they there? Is this really how they view you? Perhaps you need to check this out. If you are wrong, change the way you think of yourself. If you are right about the less than positive way they perceive you, it may be time for you to change.

The labeling exercise shows that some of the labels you give yourself are outmoded, suitable for a life you have outgrown. Of course, some labels might be correct. If you believe that they still describe you, then put the opposite word beside the negative statement you chose, and either make that a goal for change or forget about it and concentrate on your strengths.

Analyzing Your Thoughts

Look at the next section, *Negative Thinking*, and see which of these thinking styles is yours. You may have more than one favorite. This is common and certainly nothing to worry about.

Negative Thinking

The first stage is to recognize your own negative automatic thoughts. In order to identify them, keep in mind these points:

1. These thoughts just seem to come out of nowhere and flash through your mind without your being aware of them.

2. They seem very plausible at the time and you accept them as being perfectly reasonable under the circumstances, without questioning them.

3. If you challenge them with reason and facts, however, you will realize that they are illogical and unreasonable.

4. Automatic thoughts are the kinds of thoughts that most people would find depressing or anxiety-inducing if they believed them.

Wrong Labels

Anxious people will often say "I was in a complete panic," when, in fact, they were quite anxious, but nowhere near the state of extreme fear that denotes panic. Likewise, they sometimes claim, "I never slept a wink last night," when what they mean is that they had a poor night's sleep.

Using dramatic language merely makes us even more anxious and tense. It is important to describe feelings and reactions accurately, since this helps us to maintain control in a situation. Try hard to get into the habit of using accurate and realistic labels for the way you feel, and avoid dramatizing the situation unnecessarily.

All-or-Nothing Thinking

People sometimes have a tendency to see things as being a total success or a total failure when, in fact, most situations are somewhere in between. Just because something has gone wrong does not necessarily mean that the whole event is a total disaster. Try to be rational about it.

Overgeneralizing

Don't make the mistake of thinking that because you had one bad experience in a situation that all similar situations will be equally bad, or that you will always have a bad experience in similar situations. Just because you got extremely nervous meeting new people at a recent birthday party does not mean that every time you meet someone, you'll feel the same.

Exaggerating and Imagining Catastrophes

This means blowing things out of all proportion and assuming that the worst possible disaster is bound to happen in a situation you find difficult.

Thus, someone who is self-conscious about blushing might imagine a forthcoming social event in terms of blushing, everybody noticing and then criticizing or ridiculing him. The chances of this happening are, of course, remote.

Ignoring the Positive

Negative people will often overlook positive experiences during which they have coped well, or the positive aspects of a situation. So, someone who gets anxious in company might say that they only enjoy a party because they had a couple of drinks beforehand, when, in fact, this had little to do with it. Their social skills, sense of fun and enjoyment levels were more predictive of a happy outcome than the glass of wine or beer they drank.

Negatively Predicting the Future

The last stage in the downward spiral is thinking that nothing will ever happen to change things, and that the outcome is entirely bleak. In other words, "It'll all go horribly wrong."

Challenging Your Thoughts

Having identified your automatic thoughts and the thinking errors they contain, the next step is to challenge these with logic and look for alternative explanations. Much of our negative thinking is superstitious. We imagine that looking on the dark side acts as a guard against bad things happening.

An American psychologist called Seligman dispelled that notion forever. He and his team studied hundreds of people, assessing their thinking styles through watercooler banter, letters and telephone calls. He then looked them up after 25 years had passed. He discovered that the more positive thinkers were more successful in everything they undertook, had fewer nasty life events, were less likely to become depressed, and lived longer than their more negative counterparts.

We know the positive approach works, so let's get started.

First, fill in the gaps in the Sentence Completion Exercise below. Try to complete as many sentences as possible, without giving yourself problems you do not have. We will use these issues to explore different thinking styles that are much more positive in their orientation.

SENTENCE COMPLETION
ASSESSMENT OF PROBLEMS

Write down your responses to complete the sentences.

1. My biggest problem is — — — — — — — — — — — — — —

— —

2. I'm quite concerned about — — — — — — — — — — — —

— —

3. Something I do that gives me trouble is — — — — — — — — —

— —

4. Something I fail to do that gets me into trouble is — — — — — —

— —

5. A social setting I find most troublesome is — — — — — — — —

— —

6. The most frequent negative feelings in my life are — — — — — —

— —

7. These negative feelings take place when — — — — — — — — —

— —

8. The person I have most trouble with is — — — — — — — — — —

— —

9. What I find most troublesome in this relationship is — — — — — .

— —

---

10. Life would be better if __ __ __ __ __ __ __ __ __ __ __ __ __ __
__ __ __ __ __ __ __ __ __ __ __ __ __ __ __ __ __ __ __ __

11. I don't cope very well with __ __ __ __ __ __ __ __ __ __ __ __
__ __ __ __ __ __ __ __ __ __ __ __ __ __ __ __ __ __ __ __

12. What sets me most on edge is __ __ __ __ __ __ __ __ __ __ __
__ __ __ __ __ __ __ __ __ __ __ __ __ __ __ __ __ __ __ __

13. I get anxious when __ __ __ __ __ __ __ __ __ __ __ __ __ __ __
__ __ __ __ __ __ __ __ __ __ __ __ __ __ __ __ __ __ __ __

14. A value I fail to put into practice is __ __ __ __ __ __ __ __ __ __
__ __ __ __ __ __ __ __ __ __ __ __ __ __ __ __ __ __ __ __

15. I'm afraid to __ __ __ __ __ __ __ __ __ __ __ __ __ __ __ __ __
__ __ __ __ __ __ __ __ __ __ __ __ __ __ __ __ __ __ __ __

16. I wish I __ __ __ __ __ __ __ __ __ __ __ __ __ __ __ __ __ __
__ __ __ __ __ __ __ __ __ __ __ __ __ __ __ __ __ __ __ __

17. I wish I didn't __ __ __ __ __ __ __ __ __ __ __ __ __ __ __ __

18. What others dislike most about me is __ __ __ __ __ __ __ __ __ __
__ __ __ __ __ __ __ __ __ __ __ __ __ __ __ __ __ __ __ __

19. What I don't seem to handle well is __ __ __ __ __ __ __ __ __ __
__ __ __ __ __ __ __ __ __ __ __ __ __ __ __ __ __ __ __ __

20. I don't seem to have the skills I need in order to __ __ __ __ __ __
__ __ __ __ __ __ __ __ __ __ __ __ __ __ __ __ __ __ __ __

21. A problem that keeps coming back is __ __ __ __ __ __ __ __ __
__ __ __ __ __ __ __ __ __ __ __ __ __ __ __ __ __ __ __ __

22. If I could change just one thing in myself, it would be __ __ __ __
__ __ __ __ __ __ __ __ __ __ __ __ __ __ __ __ __ __ __ __

Choose one of your problems from the Sentence Completion Exercise and reality-test it below, in the section called Reality Thinking. Remember that you are reviewing your thinking about your problem.

Let us look at an example before you start. You might have said, "I lack the confidence to put myself forward for promotion." First, you must examine the evidence for insufficient confidence. What do your friends think of you? Do they think you could do the job? What about those at work? Do they think you are competent? Become a researcher into your own life. This whole process of standing back to assess your life objectively reduces years of stalled thinking and can move you on to the next stage of your career. This thinking style is especially good if you have a tendency to use old or wrong labels and tend to be an overgeneralizer. You can apply this to any situation, not just work.

Proceed with the questions below and see at the end if your thinking has shifted.

REALITY THINKING

Evidence

- What evidence is there to support your thoughts?
- What evidence is there to contradict them?

Alternative Interpretations

- How might someone else react in this situation?
- How would you advise someone else in this situation?
- What evidence is there now to support alternatives?

Effect

- What is your goal in the problems situation?
- Does the negative interpretation help or hinder you in achieving the goal?
- If you believed in an alternative, what effect would that have?

It pays to check things out. Here's an example.

Michael's Story

Michael was a solicitor who was made a partner at a young age. He would like to have been considered as an equity partner, which was the next step up, but felt that all the other partners considered him to be enough of an upstart already. He said that they often made jokes about his age, and that he lacked their wisdom. This all came out after he completed the labeling exercise, but when he was challenged to answer the questions in reality thinking, he found it difficult to separate his beliefs about himself from what his colleagues really thought.

The next day he sought feedback from his senior partners. They were incredulous that he thought he was too young, and had been waiting for him to put himself forward for promotion.

> Impossible is a word to be found only in the dictionary of fools.
> —*Napoleon Bonaparte*

Outcome Thinking

Think of another problem from the Sentence Completion Exercise. Be specific in your problem choice. Don't choose the broad term "difficult people," for example. Choose a particular person or situation. Outcome thinking is particularly good for problems that have been around for a while and that you may have felt stuck trying to resolve.

PROBLEM FRAME

Answer the following questions.

- What is your problem? _ _ _ _ _ _ _ _ _ _ _ _ _ _ _ _ _ _

- How long have you had it? _ _ _ _ _ _ _ _ _ _ _ _ _ _ _ _

- Whose fault is it? — — — — — — — — — — — — — — — —

- Who is really to blame? _ _ _ _ _ _ _ _ _ _ _ _ _ _ _ _

- What is your worst experience with this problem? — — — — — —

_ _

- Why haven't you solved it yet? _ _ _ _ _ _ _ _ _ _ _

Now, complete the outcomes box below.

OUTCOMES

- What do you want? _ _ _ _ _ _ _ _ _ _ _ _ _ _ _ _ _ _

- How will you know when you have got it? _ _ _ _ _ _ _ _ _ _

_ _

- What else in your life will improve when you get it? _ _ _ _ _ _ _

_ _

- What resources do you already have to help you achieve this outcome?

_ _

- Write down a similar goal that you succeeded in achieving:

_ _

- What do you think is the next step? _ _ _ _ _ _ _ _ _ _ _ _

_ _

Notice the difference in your experience, depending on which filter you use—i.e., problems versus results.

What differences did you notice?

_ _

_ _

_ _

_ _

_ _

_ _

_ _

_ _

If you noticed any differences in your thinking the second time, you should indulge in Outcome Thinking more often. You do not have to solve a problem in its entirety—you just have to think about the next stage. Outcome Thinking is especially good if you are one of those people who ignores the positive in situations and feels down and stuck.

The next thinking style to experiment with is Useful Thinking. This is especially good if you are prone to exaggerate and catastrophize. The table below gives you some examples of faulty thinking, less effective thinking and then useful thinking. Add your own examples, again using your problems from the Sentence Completion Exercise. Useful Thinking reveals how the language we use is important. "I will not be disorganized" still has you focusing on disorganization. It is better to say, "I am usually organized. I will be again if I take some time to put everything in its place."

> Wheresoever you go, go with all your heart.
> –Confucius

Here is one last exercise to give you a lift on a bad day. Stick it on your fridge, or on your desk at work. Read it on a bad day to give yourself a boost.

Faulty Thinking	Less Effective	Useful Thinking
I'm so nervous. I've blown it!	Don't get nervous! You'll blow it!	I feel nervous at the moment, but this is unusual; I'm normally calm and confident
I was a total failure—everyone will think I'm an idiot.	I wasn't a total failure—maybe next time.	I have succeeded to a degree—I'll build on that success next time.
I didn't get anything I wanted. I'll never do any better.	I didn't get all I wanted. I should have done it better.	I didn't get everything that I wanted, but I did get something, and that's really positive. I'm making progress.

STRENGTHS EXERCISE

Complete the following sentences:

1. One thing others like about me is _____

   _____

2. One thing I do very well is _____

   _____

3. A recent problem I've handled very well is _____

   _____

4. When I'm at my best, I _____

   _____

5. I'm glad that I _____

   _____

6. Those who know me are glad that I _____

   _____

7. A compliment that has been paid to me recently is _____

   _____

8. A value that I try hard to put into practice is _____

   _____

9. An example of my caring about others is _____

   _____

10. People can count on me to _____

    _____

11. They said I did a good job when I _____

    _____

12. Something I'm handling better this year than last is _ _ _ _ _ _ _ _ _ _ _ _

_ _

13. One thing that I've overcome is _ _ _ _ _ _ _ _ _ _ _ _ _ _ _ _ _ _

_ _

14. A good example of my ability to manage my life is _ _ _ _ _ _ _ _ _ _ _ _

_ _

15. I'm best with people when _

_ _

16. One goal I'm presently working toward is _ _ _ _ _ _ _ _ _ _ _ _ _ _ _ _

_ _

17. A recent temptation that I managed to overcome was _ _ _ _ _ _ _ _ _ _ _

_ _

18. I pleasantly surprised myself when I _ _ _ _ _ _ _ _ _ _ _ _ _ _ _ _ _ _

_ _

19. I think that I have the courage to _ _ _ _ _ _ _ _ _ _ _ _ _ _ _ _ _ _

_ _

20. If I had to say one good thing about myself, I'd say that I _ _ _ _ _ _ _ _ _

_ _

21. One way I successfully control my emotions is _ _ _ _ _ _ _ _ _ _ _ _ _ _

_ _

22. One way in which I am very dependable is _ _ _ _ _ _ _ _ _ _ _ _ _ _ _ _

_ _

23. One important thing that I intend to do within two months is _ _ _ _ _ _ _ _

_ _

CASE HISTORY

Dr. Sandra Scott has used the case histories of some of the participants in *Confidence Lab* to illustrate faulty thinking and how it affects confidence. She taught workshop members to challenge their negative thoughts, be more constructive in their thinking, and find better ways of handling their problems.

This example will help you to do the same.

Maria's Confidence Issue: Fear of Public Speaking

Maria, 39, works for the charity, Victim Support. An integral and essential part of her job is to give speeches to a variety of audiences. Maria has found this so difficult that she now avoids giving presentations, and her career is suffering. In her terror, she avoided an important training course and procrastinated over a speech for the police. Before having to give a talk (if she could not get out of it by delegating), she would withdraw from her family, become increasingly stressed, and spend her time thinking about all the things that could go wrong. Her negative thoughts would convince her that her speech would go badly, and she would ignore the fact that she had previously given a number of talks extremely well. Immediately before giving a speech, she would vomit, sometimes violently. To calm herself down, she might go to a bar to have a drink. During the talk, she would stammer, blush, sweat and forget what she wanted to say. When things were very bad, she would freeze.

All of this further confirmed her belief that she was no good at public speaking; she would think, "I'm awful at this." She would anxiously watch the audience for their response to her, hoping for a friendly face, but mostly alert for signs that things were going wrong—e.g., someone yawning or looking at their watch. Maria was so convinced that they would react badly that anything they did would be disturbing to her. On one occasion, somebody smiled and she immediately thought, "What are they smiling at—do they think I am stupid?"

If she can, she always shortens her speeches and leaves early. Maria's behavior and her response to her anxiety symptoms have affected her performance adversely, and her fears have become self-fulfilling. Her superiors have begun to notice and their response has added to her anxiety, confirming her fears and compounding the whole problem further.

Analyzing the Problem

Negative Thinking

Maria's Beliefs	Identifying the Inaccuracies
I will forget what I want to say	Negatively predicting the future
Everything will go wrong	Overgeneralizing
I will make a fool of myself	Exaggerating and fearing catastrophe
I will lose control	Negatively predicting the future
I am horrible at this	Wrong labels
Thinking about all the things that can go wrong	Negatively predicting the future
Ignoring the fact that previous speeches have gone extremely well	Ignoring the positive

Maria's Behavioral Patterns

Maria's Approach	Coping Strategies
Delegating when she can	Protective behavior— avoidance
Not doing talks when she can avoid them	
Not going on a training course	
Avoiding giving police talk	
Leaving early	Protective behavior—escape
Anxiously watching the audience	Anxiety—scanning for negative responses
Pre-performance alcohol	Ineffective coping strategies
Withdrawing from potentially supportive family	

Physiology (the body's automatic response to anxiety)

Maria's response to anxiety
Freezing
Blushing
Stammering
Sweating
Vomiting
Forgetting what to say

The Vicious Circle

Here's how Maria's thinking kept her from gaining confidence.

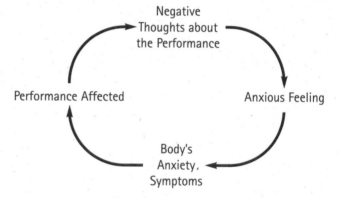

Maria's habitual response to her anxious feelings and symptoms was fueling her anxiety, which affected her performance.

Here's how we helped Maria:

- We explored her thinking and helped her to become more positive about her strengths.
- We helped her to relax.
- We taught her how to visualize success.
- We improved her vocal projection and fluency.
- She practiced presentations using "mind-mapping" (discussed in detail on pages 115–118) to prepare her content and body-language techniques, increase her confidence, and diminish her childlike behavior.

This is an example of the way in which you can break down your problem. Target the belief and behavioral aspects of your problem. The first step, however, is to see more clearly where your problem lies. You can do this by analyzing the following:

1. Build Up Your Confidence

Start by:

- Accepting you have a problem
- Motivating yourself
- Clarifying the problem
- Setting your goals for what you want to achieve
- Identifying someone to support and help you

2. Change Your Negative Beliefs

Recognize your faulty thinking by:

- Learning to examine and look at thoughts objectively.
- Picking up errors and inconsistencies in your thoughts—e.g., exaggerating, all-or-nothing thinking, ignoring the positive, overgeneralizing, and so on.
- Learning to recognize when your thoughts are inaccurate and unhelpful. Before you can change these thoughts, you must be able to identify them, and accept that they do need changing.

> I hope that I may always desire more than I can accomplish.
> *–Michelangelo Buonarroti*

Challenge your thoughts

- *Play detective*—Don't just accept your negative beliefs about yourself. Challenge them. Look for evidence for and against what you believe to be true, as you did in the labeling exercise.
- *Question yourself*—Learn to ask questions of yourself, for example: Could there be another way of looking at this? Is this logical? Is this a habit or actually a fact?
- *Play devil's advocate*—Convince yourself that your positive thoughts are winning.

Learn to push your beliefs to the fullest extent possible. If you feel you've begun to get trapped in a negative spiral, think about the problem and ask yourself, "So if my fears come true, what would that really mean?" Examine your worst-case scenario and analyze it. Ask, "Are things really that bad? What is my evidence for and against this happening?"

Replacing Inaccurate Beliefs

- Learn to generate logical, reasonable alternatives to your old beliefs
- Create an ideal scenario in your mind
- Use positive self-instruction—write down a list of positive commands you can give yourself to replace your previous anxiety-provoking ones. For example, replace, "I will lose control," with, "If things go wrong, I will remain calm." When you experience the physical symptoms of anxiety, rather than allowing these feelings to make you more anxious and thinking, "This is really going badly," try thinking, as Maria suggested, "I will remember that it is just my nervous system."

3. *Change Unhelpful Behavior*

Learning to cope with exposure—an essential part of curing your fear of speaking in public—means that you have to bite the bullet and actually do it. All else is theory. You cannot actually help yourself without doing this. You need to confront your fears and expose yourself to your anxiety. This will involve developing a hierarchy of fears, so your problem can then be approached in a graded, controlled fashion, starting with your least fearful situation and progressing to more challenging situations at your own pace. You can visualize this initially in your mind, and then in reality. Tolerating and befriending your anxiety will eventually allow you to get used to it, which will automatically lessen it and render it manageable.

Protective Behavior

Once you've exposed yourself to your anxiety, you will be tempted to resort to your previous protective behaviors. Don't do it! It prevents you from exposing yourself to your fears and learning to handle your anxiety.

4. Stop Ineffective Coping Strategies

Using stimulants like soda, coffee, tea, alcohol, cigarettes, and drugs, not eating prior to a performance to prevent nausea, and so on, must stop.

5. Develop Effective Coping Strategies

- *Role play*—Visualize and act out ideal and worst-case scenarios, and practice role reversal to test out your hypotheses.
- *Constructive feedback*—Ask your friends and colleagues for feedback and analyze your behavior yourself.
- *Communication skills*—Use them to improve your performance.
- Use *relaxation techniques*.
- *Modeling*—Learn behavior from other people, television, and reading.

POSITIVE AFFIRMATIONS

Review this chapter and write down positive statements for any thinking you wish to change.

1. Express your wishes in the present tense, as in, "I am now in the process of saving money," not, "I will save money." The idea is that you are starting the process right now, not at some future date.

2. Keep your statements positive, for example, "I feel good about myself," not, "I do not put myself down."

Note your positive statements below:

_____

_____

_____

_____

_____

_____

_____

> **QUICK REMINDERS**
>
> √ Review your thinking and note your style. If it is more negative than positive, practice alternatives: reality, outcome, and usefulness.
>
> √ Keep your Strengths Exercise close at hand to give you a boost on bad days. Review your Positive Affirmations before you go to sleep at night. This will help to counteract sneaky negative thoughts.

PROGRESS DIARY

What I've learned from this chapter	How I intend to put this into practice
1.	
2.	
3.	
4.	

EMOTION

Our emotions can be exhilarating, or they can throw us into the depths of despair. Obviously, there is a thought that precedes a feeling, but it is worth looking at emotion separately; even though it would be rare for this to happen in real life.

To be emotionally competent and confident, you need the following skills:

1. **Understanding your own emotions.** You need to recognize a feeling as it happens and have the ability to describe the way you feel. Expressing emotion does not come equally easily to everyone, unless you come from a family in which feelings are talked about openly.

2. **Recognizing emotions in others.** Empathy depends on emotional self-awareness, and is a fundamental people skill. We talked about your own body language during Day Three. This is about picking up cues and signals from others so that you can then handle them intelligently and effectively.

3. **Managing your own emotions.** Handling feelings so that they are expressed appropriately is the major skill that underpins assertiveness. In comparison to the Victorian era, emotions today are seen as good things. We see emotional repression as unhealthy. On the other hand, we can be hijacked by our emotions; this happens when strong emotion overcomes all attempts at rationality, and we end up saying things that are career-limiting or just plain damaging to another person. Talking about how we feel in a calm fashion so that solutions can be reached is the subject of Day Five.

4. Handling relationships. Fostering long-term relationships requires great skill in managing emotions in others. People who excel in these skills have good marriages that last and friendships that span decades. They do well at anything that relies upon interacting smoothly with other people.

So let's start with The Emotional Language Exercise. This will help you understand your own emotions and, as a result, those of others. Describe what you feel when you experience these emotions. Choose those that you instinctively respond to—for example, you may feel instant discomfort, conflict, or anxiety when you see certain words, or just have a general feeling that they exert a powerful influence over you.

Two examples are included to help you. They describe possible feelings associated with anger and love.

Take a look at the following examples:

Anger	**Love**
When I feel angry:	*When I love someone:*
I can feel confused	I feel exhilarated
I feel hot and bothered	I feel glowing
I feel instantly vindictive	I can feel confident
I want to do something about it now, although I know that would be disastrous	I can feel vulnerable
	I can feel less in control of my life
I can feel hurt	I feel generous
I can feel rejected	

EMOTIONAL LANGUAGE EXERCISE

Here is a list of emotions for you to describe:

1. Accepted	8. Jealous	15. Hopeful
2. Afraid	9. Loving	16. Inferior
3. Angry	10. Satisfied	17. Joyful
4. Anxious	11. Defensive	18. Lonely
5. Attracted	12. Free	19. Rejected
6. Competitive	13. Frustrated	20. Trusting
7. Intimate	14. Guilty	

Write your choice emotions and descriptions below:

_____

_____

_____

_____

_____

_____

_____

_____

_____

_____

_____

_____

_____

_____

_____

If you've ever thought that emotions were for wimps, then it is a good idea to practice your new emotional competence as often as possible. The ability to talk directly about how you feel is the most powerful communication tool you can possess. A good place to start is the positive expression of emotion in the form of rewards and compliments. To help, we are going to talk about the concept of "stroking."

Stroking

If you would like the people around you to be more appreciative of your endeavors, then you must appreciate them. Stroking comes from the idea that when we were young, our parents hugged and stroked us. Not only did this make us feel secure, but it encouraged our development by providing us with feedback from our environment.

However, as we grow older, we get fewer hugs, but our desire for feedback does not diminish. As adults we cannot go around asking for strokes indiscriminately. (Well, we could, but not without sending the wrong message.) So, strokes become metaphorical, which means that we receive them through words of thanks, a gift, a wave or a smile. Stroking can also mean a satisfying of the senses through color, texture, sound, touch and taste. All of these actually constitute positive strokes.

Types of Stroking

Negative stroking is about belittling people, ignoring or putting them down. Negative strokes should not to be confused with criticism, which can be very positive and helpful if delivered in a constructive way. Negative strokes discount people and help to make them feel inadequate. Self-confidence is eroded, not built up.

Examples of Negative Strokes

- Keeping people waiting
- Not consulting or involving people in decisions that affect them
- Asking for suggestions when you are already clear on your decision
- Hurrying people up rather than listening to them
- Closing an issue before everyone feels heard
- Overexplaining the obvious and patronizing listeners as if they were incapable of grasping the problem themselves
- Being condescending
- Refusing to acknowledge someone's expressed feelings
- Using jargon
- Name-dropping

Examples of Positive Strokes

- Being on time
- Consulting people when decisions have an impact on them
- Collaborating when new ideas are required
- Taking time to listen to what people have to say
- Rewarding people verbally or with gifts or a pat on the back
- Acknowledging people's feelings
- Using language everyone can understand
- Making people feel valued and important
- Smiling and nodding encouragement

When people undermine themselves, saying things like, "I don't know much about this, but. . ." or, "It was nothing really," they have probably been exposed to negative strokes at home or at work. They have internalized the put-downs and almost want to belittle themselves before anyone else does. Praising people who are like this can be difficult, as they tend to reject compliments. Their embarrassment shouldn't stop you from doing it, however. They simply need to get used to being rewarded rather than punished.

Strokes are:

- about recognition
- the ways we demonstrate our awareness of the existence of another human being
- a biological necessity—although the level of stroking needed varies between individuals and situations

Positive strokes:

- are life- and growth-encouraging
- invite the recipients to feel okay about themselves and others

Negative strokes:

- discourage certain behaviors
- invite the recipients to feel dissatisfied about their behavior and invite them to change

Strokes (cont.)

Unconditional strokes are:
- given for just existing
- about something over which we have no control
- about you as a person

Conditional strokes are:
- given for doing something specific
- about something over which we have control
- about an aspect of our behavior, e.g., work performance

Strokes are given and received via the senses:

Hearing—The things we say to each other, the sounds of music, singing; tone of voice (angry or friendly, for example).

Sight—Facial expressions, gestures, postures; paintings, ornaments, scenery; written comments (such as memos or performance appraisals).

Touch—Shaking hands, holding, hitting, textures, and temperatures.

Taste and Smell—Through food and drink, perfumes, air fresheners, tobacco.

Individuals develop characteristic patterns of stroking. Complete the Stroking Patterns Exercise on the next page to assess your pattern.

STROKING PATTERNS EXERCISE

At the top of each column, note down the names of six people with whom you have had close contact recently—three at work (one should be a boss) and three at home. Consider when you have given and received strokes.

Names						
Write down the last time you gave this person a significant stroke						
Was the stroke positive or negative?						
What prompted it?						
When did you last receive a stroke from them?						
Was that positive or negative?						
What prompted it?						

How Do You Stroke?

Afterward, review your answers and become more aware of the ways in which you give and receive strokes. Consider first your choice of six people. Are they a representative cross-section, or have you included only those people you like most, and therefore choose to reward most? What interactions do you have, or do you not have, with the colleagues you like least? To be professional, you need to reward performance whether you like a colleague or not. Have you included your boss? Sometimes we forget to stroke people in authority. They are human, too, despite perhaps having more status or being paid more than you.

Next, review your responses in the section entitled Giving Strokes. How do you appear to others? How much time is spent in put-downs compared to positives? Note that constructive criticism is a positive stroke—it implies that the person can do better, and that you care enough about them to let them know how.

How do you receive strokes? Are you getting a reasonable quantity? Or is there a lot of joking and put-downs among your friends, so that genuine praise is outlawed? When someone does pay you a compliment, do you reward it by saying, "Thank you," instead of putting yourself down?

Do you stroke more at work or at home, and where do you receive the majority of your strokes? You are probably taking for granted people whom you stroke less. And if you can't remember when you last gave a stroke to anybody, then start immediately as if your life really depends on it. It probably does.

Celebrate Winning

Write down at least six ideas to celebrate winning. They should be entirely personal strokes, rewarding yourself for an achievement or completion of a project. If you work in a team, write down things you can do together to mark success. Be sure that these ideas are original, and you have never used them before.

Life is so hectic that we have barely finished one project before we have to embark upon another. Closure and the reinforcement of success raise morale and are therefore vitally important.

> **Note your ideas here to celebrate winning:**
>
> _
>
> _
>
> _
>
> _
>
> _

Dealing with Difficult People

Nothing increases confidence more than the knowledge that you can go anywhere, do anything, and cope with anyone. The last part of Day Five will concentrate on skills for handling a difficult person (or people) in your life and ways in which you can deal effectively with any anger and conflict that arises.

Everyone knows someone they find difficult or have found difficult in the past. So who is your difficult person?

Think of an experience you have had with a difficult person, for example, someone who did not do as you asked, who was aggressive or dismissive toward you, or who generally gets under your skin.

Now you are going to learn to deal with them effectively through The Four-Step Process.

Step 1—Analyze People and Situations

Write down what it is that your difficult person does to be difficult. In other words, describe the behavior that gets up your nose. Then, with that in mind, ask yourself what they want out of behaving that way. Do they, or did they, want power or prestige or something else entirely? Reflect on your interactions and become a psychological sleuth.

> **THE FOUR-STEP PROCESS FOR DEALING WITH DIFFICULT PEOPLE**
>
> **Step 1.** Analyze people and situations
>
> **Step 2.** Stroke your difficult person
>
> **Step 3.** Negotiate
>
> **Step 4.** Assert yourself

ANALYZING YOUR DIFFICULT PERSON

What do they do to be difficult?

_____

_____

_____

_____

_____

What do difficult people want?

_____

_____

_____

_____

_____

This exercise should help you to understand the difficult person better, and also realize that, while their behavior might be bad, their motivation may be genuine. They may want a perfect report or to have their say, but they are just going about it badly. They probably have not had the privilege of being part of *Confidence Lab*.

Of course, we rarely give that difficult person what they want. In fact we would rather go out of our way not to than to do that. The trouble with this strategy is that the difficult person just gets more difficult as their goals for status or consideration are not met. However, we will get back to that later. Let's turn our attention to you.

BOX	TRIANGLE	RECTANGLE	CIRCLE	SQUIGGLE
Office				
Every pencil in place	Status symbols	Mishmash	Comfortable	Messy
	Awards	Imitator	Homelike	Bleak
Computer	Powerful	Disorganized	Plants	Dramatic
Body Language				
Stiff	Composed	Clumsy	Relaxed	Animated
Controlled	Jaunty	Nervous	Smiling	Theatrical
Poker face	Piercing eyes	Fleeting eyes	Direct eyes	Mercurial
Nervous laugh	Pursed mouth	Giggle	Full laugh	Sexual cues
High-pitched voice	Power voice	High-pitched voice	Mellow voice	Fast talker
Twitches	Solid physique	Silent	Talkative	Mannerisms
Slow movements	Smooth moves	Jerky moves	Head nods	Fast moves
Precise gestures	Large gestures	Flushed face	Excessive	No touch
Perspiration			Touching	High energy
			Attractive	
Personal habits				
Loves routine	Interrupts	Forgetful	Easy going	Spontaneous
Put in writing	Game-player	Nervous	Joiner	Disorganized
Always prompt	Early-arriver	Late or early	Hobbies	Rebellious
Neat	Joke-teller	Outbursts	Sloppy	Works alone
Planner	Power	Avoids	Good cook	Life of party
Precise	Handshake	Variety	Patriotic	Daydreams
Collector	Fidgety	Blurts out	TV watcher	Interrupts
Social loner	Addictions		Socializer	Fickle

What the Psycho-Geometric Test Reveals

This test reveals just how easily conflicts can arise.

Circles and triangles do not always see eye-to-eye.

Triangles can be annoyed by a circle's humanitarian zeal and people orientation. "But what is it costing?" is the cry of the triangle.

A box living or working with a squiggle can quickly be at odds.

A box will want everything in its place, whereas squiggles do not even see the places. Everything is everywhere. "Filing? Don't be stupid, that's what floors are for," the squiggle would exclaim, which drives the box crazy.

Rectangles, almost without fail, are in transition.

Forget about the other descriptions. It is their state of flux or indecision about the way ahead in their lives that is their major characteristic. It can be an exciting time for rectangles as they explore a variety of options.

Your second choice modifies your first.

If you are a box first choice and a circle second, then you are a sociable, organized person—not always an obvious combination!

For a marriage or a team at work to function well, it is useful to have a variety of different people and therefore shapes.

A team of squiggles hardly bears contemplation. Having twenty ideas a minute may be exciting, but not if no one is organized enough to put them into practice.

Step 2—Stroke Your Difficult Person

If you are forever wishing that your tormenting frog were a prince or princess, you are wasting valuable time that you could be using for problem-solving. Moaning serves no purpose. Using strategies that are designed to minimize purposeless behavior is what it's all about.

What makes it possible to cope with difficult people at all is that, like everyone else, they have positive responses in their repertoire. If you can avoid saying or doing those things that give rise to negative behavior and encourage more productive responses, then you will cope more successfully with that individual. So look for the good and ignore the bad. Stroke every response that is positive, and you will get more positive responses. Here's an example.

How a Little Goes a Long Way

A female executive realized that she expected compliments from the men with whom she worked. She rarely gave them in return. So one day, she complimented the Chief Executive on his tie and he wore it for a week. The tie may have been a little soup-stained by Friday, but now she knew just how well her "stroke" had worked.

Step 3—Negotiate

Perhaps your relationship with your difficult person has gone beyond the stage of being amenable to the occasional reward, so the next step is one of negotiation.

> They can because they think they can.
> –Virgil

Below is a technique that was first used during the S.A.L.T. peace talks. It is now the strategy of choice for world peace treaties, so it should be good enough for our much pettier disputes. The whole idea is that before wading in with what we want out of the discussions, we should consider the other person's agenda and what they might want.

The Balcony Negotiation

The Americans, all those years back, would brainstorm what they wanted from the next part of the talks and try to verbally batter the Russians into submission. On the other side of the hotel courtyard where they were staying, they could see the Russians on their balcony doing the same. This was the old unionized way of negotiation, but they had been doing it that way for years and were more than a little weary.

Then one of the diplomats had a great idea. He suggested working out in advance what the Russians wanted rather than what they, the Americans, wanted and deciding what they would in the end have to give them. So, much to the astonishment of the Russians, the Americans returned after their break, agreed to about 80 of the items under discussion and ended up talking about two instead of 102.

Gorbachev and Reagan were suddenly shaking hands on the White House lawn after years of Cold War peace talks. So here is the strategy for you to experiment with in your own Confidence Lab. Use the Balcony Negotiation to help you create a mental image so that you will remember the technique.

How the Balcony Negotiation Works

The Balcony Negotiation is structured around the following four steps.

1. Go to the balcony

Go to the discussions with your difficult person with a very clear idea of what you want out of the meeting. It is all too easy to get side-tracked when there is personal enmity around.

2. Step to their side

Step to their side of the balcony first, and acknowledge what might be in the discussions for them, be it financial gain for a "triangular" boss, an easy life for a lazy employee, or a bit of respect for a warring parent.

3. Invite them to step to your side

Talk to them about what you want out of the discussions. Take along as much information as possible so they can make a decision there and then.

4. Build a connecting bridge

Start discussing a compromise between what you want and what they have to gain.

The WIFT Factor

The power of the Balcony is the WIFT factor—this means, "what's in it for them." For you to win, you must help them get what they want, too. You must motivate them first, or they will actively block your ideas. Try it out on your difficult person and monitor the results.

One last thought on this: if you are trying to negotiate a wage raise, a bank loan or a new computer, you will need a number of strategies for your argument. Bosses, especially, can say no easily if it involves financial outlay. You must have a number of arguments up your sleeve if you are going to get what you want. Most of them should be WIFT factors with good financial backup and literature. It is easy to counter one argument, but much more difficult to keep refusing your fourth then fifth proposition. They then know you mean business.

Step 4—Assert Yourself

You may feel that you have tried all that has been suggested so far—and got nowhere. Help is at hand in the shape of something called the DESC script. But first, let's see how you handle your anger, because it's likely that your difficult person, if he has resisted your strategies so far, is driving you slowly mad.

Complete the following Anger Test, giving examples of when you reacted in the ways asked.

> ### THE ANGER TEST
> 1. When do I usually decide to keep my anger quiet?
>
> 2. When do I usually walk away from the other person when I'm angry?
>
> 3. When have I simmered for days and then vented my anger in a big blow up?
>
> 4. When do I appear to be hurt when I'm actually angry?
>
> 5. When do I take my anger out on someone other than the person who caused the anger?
>
> 6. When have I expressed my anger directly and firmly, but without calling the other person names?

The trick of handling that persistently difficult person is to remain cool, calm and collected. If you remember back to the PAC checklist you completed on Day Two, it was the adult mode, without the emotional baggage you bring from your background, that won the day.

The DESC script helps you to be objective even in the face of the most irrational person. It looks deceptively simple but keeps you on track to communicate clearly what they have been doing, how you feel about it, what you want them to do now, and the consequences of their not making that change. Anyone will take you seriously if you handle them directly like this. Of course, there are no guarantees, but you will be very effective.

THE DESC SCRIPT

Describe the situation

Express how you feel

Specify what you want

Consequences which will result, positive or negative

A Tale of Two Sisters

Two sisters had always had a rather stormy relationship, but when Sheila, the younger of the two, went to live in London, they thought that some distance would help. After Sheila was ensconced in her flat, Julia made trips to London to visit friends and, of course, stayed with her sister. Julia had the habit of inviting her friends to Sheila's flat. Raucous parties would ensue, to which Sheila was never invited. In the morning, there was the mess to clear up, as Julia and her friends never did it. Normally, what happened was that Sheila would act the silent martyr, cleaning up, but making large sighs.

Having learned the DESC Script, Sheila decided to do things differently. She sat her sister down the morning after the party and told her about the situation, how she felt, what she wanted and what would happen if they did not come to some an agreement. Calmly, she relayed to Julia that it was not just the untidiness she minded but that she was never asked to join in. She said that she got all the mess without the enjoyment and, if this continued, Julia would not be invited back. Julia was dumbfounded. Her sister had never talked to her like that before. She apologized profusely and next time she included her sister in the festivities and organized an army of friends to clean up.

From Julia's point of view, she thought that her sister disliked her friends and so did not invite her to their parties. And she had meant to clean up, but Sheila was always there first, playing the martyr.

As a result of using the DESC Script, the sisters are now communicating and are much better friends.

Emotional Coaching

Instilling wisdom is best carried out through a coaching process. Sporting analogies and sports heroes abound to help managers train their teams to be more proficient. I could never see the relevance myself and was quite delighted to hear David Gower say at a dinner once that he could find no parallels between sports and business. However, as he was paid handsomely to supply motivational speeches at conferences, he was also happy to draw as many comparisons as it took.

Coaching, training, making things happen—this is all made easier with motivated, happy people. However, people do have problems and they are not always willing and able to learn. Remember, the test is how you handle the bad times and turn them into the good. And key to that is how you cope with the variety of emotions that are hurled at you.

Complete the Emotional Coaching questionnaire below. Be honest. Answer the questions according to what you actually do at the moment, not what you might aspire to do. You can analyze the results starting on page 102.

EMOTIONAL COACHING QUESTIONNAIRE

1. People really have very little to be sad about.   True False Don't know

2. I think that anger is okay as long as it's under control.   True False Don't know

3. People acting sad are just trying to get you to feel sorry for them.   True False Don't know

4. If someone gets angry, they should be excluded.   True False Don't know

5. When people are acting unhappy, they are real pests.   True False Don't know

6. Stress is good for you.   True False Don't know

7. When people are unhappy, I am expected to fix the world.   True False Don't know

8. I spend a lot of time helping staff sort out their stress problems.   True False Don't know

9.	I really have no time for sadness in my life.	True	False	Don't know
10.	Anger is a dangerous state.	True	False	Don't know
11.	If you ignore someone's unhappiness, it tends to go away and take care of itself.	True	False	Don't know
12.	Everyone has got to have some stress in their lives.	True	False	Don't know
13.	Anger usually means aggression.	True	False	Don't know
14.	Feelings are private and not public.	True	False	Don't know
15.	When you notice signs of stress, you need to inter-vene quickly to help.	True	False	Don't know
16.	I don't mind dealing with someone's unhappiness, as long as it doesn't last too long.	True	False	Don't know
17.	Helping staff cope with conflict is one of my managerial roles.	True	False	Don't know
18.	I prefer a happy person to someone who is overly emotional.	True	False	Don't know
19.	It's all right to show you're stressed.	True	False	Don't know
20.	When someone is unhappy, it's a time to problem-solve.	True	False	Don't know
21.	I help people get over unhappiness quickly so they can move on to better things.	True	False	Don't know
22.	I don't see someone's stress as an opportunity to learn much.	True	False	Don't know
23.	I think that, when people are depressed, they have over emphasized the negatives in life.	True	False	Don't know
24.	In my view, anger is natural, like clearing your throat.	True	False	Don't know
25.	When someone is acting angrily, they are very unpleasant.	True	False	Don't know
26.	I set limits on people's anger.	True	False	Don't know
27.	When someone acts stressed, it's to get attention.	True	False	Don't know
28.	Anger is an emotion worth exploring.	True	False	Don't know
29.	I try to change people's angry moods into cheerful ones.	True	False	Don't know

30. Getting angry is like letting off steam, releasing the pressure.   True   False   Don't know

31. When someone is unhappy, it's a chance to get closer.   True   False   Don't know

32. People really have very little to be stressed about.   True   False   Don't know

33. When someone is unhappy, I try to help them explore what is causing it.   True   False   Don't know

34. People get overanxious if you leave them alone.   True   False   Don't know

35. It is important to find out why someone is unhappy.   True   False   Don't know

36. When people are depressed, I'm worried they have negative personalities.   True   False   Don't know

37. If there's a lesson I've learned about unhappiness, it's that it is okay to express it.   True   False   Don't know

38. I'm not sure anything can be done to change unhappiness.   True   False   Don't know

39. When someone is unhappy, I'm not quite sure what they want me to do.   True   False   Don't know

40. Stress is such an overused word; people just use it as an excuse.   True   False   Don't know

41. If there's a lesson I have learned about anger, it's that it's okay to express it.   True   False   Don't know

42. When someone is angry, I try to be understanding of their mood.   True   False   Don't know

43. When someone is angry, I'm not quite sure what they want me to do.   True   False   Don't know

44. When someone is angry, I want to know what they are thinking.   True   False   Don't know

45. When someone is stressed and anxious, I just feel they are not coping well.   True   False   Don't know

46. When someone is angry, I try to let them know I care, no matter what.   True   False   Don't know

47. When someone is angry, I put myself in their shoes.   True   False   Don't know

48. It's important to help a person find out what caused the anger.   True   False   Don't know

Interpreting the Results

Dismissing

Add up the number of times you said "true" to the following questions:

1, 2, 7, 9, 11, 16, 18, 21, 22, 23, 29, 32   Total ☐

Disapproving

Add up the number of times you said "true" to the following questions:

3, 4, 5, 10, 13, 14, 25, 26, 27, 36, 40, 45   Total ☐

Laissez-Faire

Add up the number of times you said "true" to the following questions:

8, 15, 17, 20, 28, 31, 33, 35, 42, 44, 47, 48   Total ☐

Emotional Coaching

Add up the number of times you said "true" to the following questions:

6, 12, 19, 24, 30, 34, 37, 38, 39, 41, 43, 46   Total ☐

If you responded "don't know" more than four times to any group of these questions, you may want to work at becoming more aware of emotion in yourself and in others.

Now compare your four scores. The higher your score in any one area, the greater your tendency to respond to anger in that way.

Analyzing Your Results

The ideal score would be zero in the dismissing and disapproving categories, with a high score for emotional coaching, and a peppering of scores in the laissez-faire category.

To dismiss or disapprove of another's upset or anger is to force the emotion to become subterranean. When this happens, all sorts of strange behaviors ensue, with the pursuit of hidden agendas, and the scapegoating of others. People very swiftly determine whether it is wise to be emotionally honest, or if they should just pretend to be inscrutable.

High scores in the laissez-faire category mean that you are happy to have emotion expressed around you, but don't necessarily feel you have to intervene to understand or sort it out. A high score here is fine, but it should not be your highest. It should be coupled with an equally high, if not higher, emotional coaching score.

When emotion is expressed, it means that people care. They may not express it well, and the language used may be aggressive, but, where there's emotion, there's life. Dealing with these feelings moves you, your group, and the organization forward.

You don't have to become a therapist to be an emotional coach. If the problem is beyond your expertise, you can get guidance from a professional. Most emotional coaching starts with the question, "Why?" For example, "Why do you feel that way?" or, "Why do you get stressed about deadlines?" or, "Why have you been feeling low?"

Become an emotional coach for all emotions expressed, not just those with which you feel comfortable. A head of education, when he contemplated emotional coaching, said that he could understand all emotions except depression. He expected anyone to be over his or her depression in three weeks—any longer, and he felt they were "stringing it out."

> The best way out is always through.
> –Robert Frost

THE ANIMAL EXERCISE

Look at the animals on the next page and follow these instructions:

1. Choose the animal you admire most, and write below what attributes you admire.

2. Choose your next favorite animal and, in the space provided, write what you like about it.

3. Make a third choice, and write again the adjectives to describe your choice.

4. For your last choice, write down what you dislike about this animal, and anything that you fear about it.

THE ANIMAL EXERCISE

_____

_____

_____

_____

_____

_____

_____

_____

_____

_____

How to Interpret Your Animals

Look at the adjectives you have used. Then:

1. Look for any repetitions. These words are important to you, and describe values that you hold dear.

2. Identify any emotional words, because these are things that you are passionate about.

3. Finally, look at the adjectives to describe the animals you dislike. These describe areas of you life that you wish to avoid.

How Animals Help You Change

For example, one young woman chose the squirrel and the eagle, then the dolphin. The words that she used most often to describe these creatures were freedom, speed, responsiveness, agility, and vision. The last animal on her agenda was the bear, which she saw as lumbering, big and inflexible. This helped her to realize that although her family were keen for her to move up the career ladder, she wasn't ready. Instead, she decided to spread her own wings and take a year off to go traveling.

CASE HISTORY

Mark's Confidence Issue: Fear of Showing His Softer Side

Mark is a 35-year-old ex-boxer who is now a bricklayer, married with six children. With his muscular build and close-shaven head, Mark looks tough, and not a man to be messed with. He is not unlike his hero, *EastEnders'* Grant Mitchell. Mark deliberately created his macho image, despite the fact that he believes that it gives people the impression he is a cold, hard person. He feels he needs this image to act as a protective shell to hide his real self. Inside, he considers the real him to be a softie. He is creative and emotional, and writes poetry. However, Mark lacks the confidence to be his real self, or to show his emotions to the people who know him. He thinks that if he does, his friends would think he is a sissy and probably laugh. He hides the truth from them, and says he is writing plays rather than poetry. He also believes that, without his "armor," he would be vulnerable and get pushed around.

> That feeling by which the mind embarks in great honorable courses with a sure hope and trust in itself.
> —*Cicero*

These beliefs stem from an incident that occurred on his first day of high school. Another boy threw a brick at him and Mark felt that he did this because he looked vulnerable. The incident acted as a trigger for him to change his image and toughen up, so he developed his protective macho shell. Now this shell makes it hard for him to share his emotions with his loved ones; he tends to bottle them up. He believes his children think he's strict and hard on them. His wife is unsure if he loves her or not and his lack of emotion frustrates her and affects their relationship. He had moved away from his old neighborhood, and the people he knows, hoping he would be free to be himself. He has realized, however, that what he really needs is the confidence to lose his tough-as-nails image, allowing himself to do what "macho Mark" would not dare do.

Analyzing Mark's Problem
Negative Thoughts (unhelpful beliefs and faulty thinking)

Mark's Beliefs	Identifying the Inaccuracies
If I'm not hard, then I'll appear vulnerable	All-or-nothing thinking
Friends think I am a sissy	Wrong labels
People laugh at me	
People think I am cold-hearted	
My children think I am hard and strict	
Vulnerable people get picked on	Negative predictions
This stems from an incident that occurred once	Overgeneralizing
Hides his real self in a macho shell	Poor self-esteem

Mark's Behavioral Patterns

Mark's Approach	Coping Strategies
Bottles up his emotions	Ineffective coping strategies
Deliberately created macho image	
Hides his real self	
Moved from the area	Protective behavior— avoidance
Hides the truth	Protective behavior—escape

Here's how we helped Mark:

- We gave him practical coaching in effective voice projection
- We encouraged him to express his vulnerability through his poetry with the group
- We helped him to realize that not only was no one laughing at him, but they liked him even more for expressing his emotions
- We helped him recognize that his "macho" image only served to prevent him from being himself
- In expressing his early negative experience of being bullied, Mark saw that his reactions, while appropriate then, were inappropriate now that he was an adult
- We gave him useful scripts to use when talking to people

QUICK REMINDERS

√ Remember to recognize your emotions and those of others. This will help you to manage your own feelings, and empathize with others.

√ Give yourself and others "strokes" (see pages 84–88).

√ Use the Four-Step Process for handling difficult people, whoever they may be. Remember, this can be your mom or your boss.

√ Get everyone you know to do the Psycho-Geometric Test (see pages 91–94). It always goes down well, and will give you a greater insight into the way they tick, and how best to handle them.

√ When you are in the midst of difficult discussions, then use the Balcony Negotiation (see pages 95–97). Again, this is equally useful when negotiating with your errant teenage daughter or with your mortgage lender.

√ When you next feel angry, turn it to your advantage by being assertive, using the DESC script model (see pages 97–98). Try it the next time you get cold or inedible food at a restaurant and your waiter/waitress doesn't take you seriously!

√ Reward the people around you eight times more than you criticize them if you want them to feel good about themselves.

PROGRESS DIARY

What I've learned from this chapter	How I intend to put this into practice
1.	
2.	
3.	
4.	

ACTION

Day Six is action day. Today we are going to explain a fool-proof way to meet new people and know what to say. You'll also learn a great method of dealing with the most dull dinner-party guest or business associate with whom you have nothing in common.

We are also going to show you how to put together a presentation for a board meeting, a best man's speech, or a vote of thanks at the Women's Institute. The principles are the same for all. You will learn how to prepare it in five minutes, if necessary, and deliver it confidently.

> It takes three weeks to replace an old habit with a new skill and another nine weeks to turn that new skill into a new habit.
>
> So get started!

Of course, since this is action day, it is about doing things, and doing things differently. The exercises are straightforward, but you must practice them. Changing your behavior is not easy. It won't happen automatically, just as a result of reading this book and putting strategies into practice

MEETING NEW PEOPLE

When you lack confidence, meeting new people can be a nightmare. Because of anxiety, the fear of being tongue-tied can make you go weak at the knees. The way to get over this is to have a plan of action.

Imagine, for a minute, that you always knew what to say, were never stuck for words and everyone thought you were just the best conversationalist. Well, the key to success lies in FORE. If you ask people you meet questions in FORE areas, you will get to know them in five minutes. And, more important than that, you will make friends.

FORE provides you with a structure of common things to discuss with anyone. Most people have or have had a family, and an occupation. They will probably have some kind of hobby, even if it is just watching television. And all of us have had to be educated.

Lack of confidence makes us imagine that we have to do the talking and come up with hilarious stories and riveting chat. In fact, the trick is to get the other person talking so that all we have to do is listen and respond occasionally. They will, of course, think that we are wonderful conversationalists, because we make them feel important.

There is a skill in asking questions. Closed questions like, "Do you...?" or, "Have you...?" can be answered by yes or no. This discourages discussion. What you want is an easy, relaxing time, so open-ended questions are preferable.

FORE
F = family
O = occupation
R = recreation
E = education

TYPES OF QUESTIONS

Closed	Open	Probing
Are?	What?	How?
Do?	Which?	In what way?
Have?	When?	Tell me more.
	Where?	Describe in more detail
	Who?	For what reasons?
	Why?	

When you try out FORE today—and it should be today—then do experiment with open-ended questions. Don't be concerned if it takes a little while to get used to them, especially if you've had a lifetime of asking closed ones and receiving monosyllabic answers.

If you really want to bond, then probing questions are for you. Saying, "That's really interesting, tell me more about that," is very captivating. This technique will have people chatting to you all night, so be sure you are genuinely interested in them. If you are only pretending, then you may get cornered by the party bore, who now adores you because you've shown so much interest in him!

Dealing with a Boring Person

Not everyone you meet will be scintillating company. So, what can you do if you are, for example, stuck with them at dinner for two or three hours?

What you need to know about is the Emotional Bank.

THE EMOTIONAL BANK

1. Discover interest
Ask open-ended questions until you find something in common, or a topic that is slightly more interesting.

2. Build a credit balance
Boring people are rarely attended to and seldom rewarded, so when you reward the interesting bits, people are usually only too delighted to run with those topics.

3. Deposit
You can offer information yourself, ask questions, or move the topic to more interesting territory. For example, if someone is droning on about football, then you can subtly ask about the drunken/sexual exploits of the stars. Much more interesting!

Become experimental with the relationships around you and you will have no time to be shy and retiring. There are just too many interesting people to talk to.

But you do have to practice FORE on anyone that moves—at bus stops, stations, airports, anywhere. It must become second nature, like breathing. Life will never be dull again and you will meet great people. You will be given things, too. For example, a friend who flies a lot always chats to the stewards. He asks where they live, what their shifts are like and where they enjoy flying to. He always ends up with two meals, headphones, and miniatures of gin and whisky, whether he wants them or not.

Putting FORE into practice

During *Confidence Lab* at dinner one evening, Jane and Mark were given homework. They had to talk to at least two people and ask them questions from FORE. Both of them had been very shy at the initial cocktail party, standing back on the periphery of the group. So it was not an easy task for either of them.

Jane took to FORE like a duck to water and was seen initiating con- versations left and right. Mark found the exercise more of a chal- lenge, as he found it difficult to break into existing discussions. However, he was more involved and animated than ever before, just waiting to ask his questions. This is something Mark needs to work on after *Confidence Lab*.

PRESENTATION SKILLS

We have all heard that surveys of things we most fear rank pub- lic speaking ahead of more permanent things, such as death. So it's evident that a majority of people would rather die than speak in front of others. It doesn't have to be this way—especially since the ideas we are going to talk about can make presenta- tions stress-free, whomever they might be to, from the mother- and-toddler group to 2,000 business people.

WHAT MAKES A GOOD SPEAKER?

	Positively agree	Agree	Disagree	Strongly Disagree
1. What you say in a presentation is the most important element.	☐	☐	☐	☐
2. You always need to be anxious to keep on your toes and deliver an effective presentation.	☐	☐	☐	☐
3. How you look when presenting is a major influencing for an audience.	☐	☐	☐	☐
4. Perfecting a good presentation means that you don't have to change it for each audience.	☐	☐	☐	☐
5. Humor and stories are out of place in a formal presentation.	☐	☐	☐	☐
6. Reading your notes is important, as it means that you leave nothing out of your presentation.	☐	☐	☐	☐
7. Mistakes ruin a good presentation.	☐	☐	☐	☐
8. Enthusiasm for your subject will generally see you through.	☐	☐	☐	☐

In Truth

1. What you say is not the most important element. It is much more likely to be how you look—whether you are animated, smiling, and generally engaging. This is reassuring to know, as it is so easy to worry about remembering every word of a presentation.

2. It is so much better if you are relaxed during your presentation. Then you can attend to the audience, not your sweating palms!

3. How you look is essential and, as explained in question 1, one of the real keys to success.

4. Every presentation you give should be targeted at your audience and, therefore, different every time.

5. Humor and stories are fabulous in any presentation—surprisingly even at a funeral.

6. Never read notes. The spoken and the written word come from different planets and shouldn't be confused with each other. If you leave something out, who will know except you?

7. Making mistakes is not important; recovery is. Everyone makes mistakes and it can be quite endearing not to be seen as perfect. The trick is not to be thrown off balance and to appear in control.

8. Enthusiasm is essential. Without it, you are better to delegate the presentation to someone who is passionate about the subject.

The Bottom Line

People buy people. It is a fact that, if you are liked, your ideas will stand a better chance of success. Remember, you have 30 seconds to make a good impression.

You are your best visual aid. During a presentation, your audience has plenty of time to assess you. Do you look the best you can, or have you been flung together? Be positive about your attributes. If you are not, who will be?

Enthusiasm conquers all (well, almost all). Are you a user-friendly presenter, with an animated, friendly face and lively speech? If not, read on for helpful pointers. **Remember, good presenters are made, not born.**

Let's find out what you think makes a confidence speaker.

You will find the magic formula for putting together a presentation in the right margin. Once you know how to follow this, presentations almost write themselves.

1. Researching

You need to know whom you are presenting to so that you can target your talk to suit your audience. Telephone in advance, and ask the following questions:

RESEARCH CHECKLIST

√ Who will be there? What are the backgrounds of those attending? Will they know anything about the subject you will be presenting?

√ How many will attend? Is it five or 50? You need to make sure your visual aids will work, and can be seen clearly from the back of the room.

√ Where will your talk be held? Will it be after dinner or lunch at the table, or on a platform?

√ What equipment will you need, and do they have it?

Unfortunately, there are stories of many people who did not do their research. One consultant, for example, turned up at a meeting which she thought five people were attending. Imagine her consternation when she opened the door to find 500! Actually, she closed it again, thinking she had gone to the wrong place—not a good start, or a confident entrance.

2. Mind-Mapping

We mistakenly believe that normal sentences are the best way to remember what we are going to say. In fact, 90 percent of words are not useful when you're trying to memorize a presentation.

In 1974, Tony Buzan launched the concept of mind maps. He discovered that the brain works better when we don't have to remember sentences with all the ands and buts. Rather than starting at the top of a page and working down in sentences and lists, what we should do is start with a main idea in the center and then branch out with ideas.

THE MAGIC FORMULA

1. Researching

2. Mind-mapping

3. Structuring

4. Topping and tailing

ADVANTAGES OF MIND MAPS

- Mind-mapping echoes the way we think—literally, all over the place!
- It allows us to be more creative, because we do not impose a structure on our thinking.
- New information can be added easily, and it doesn't involve writing it in margins.
- Mind maps help us to memorize key points.
- Mind-mapping is great for brainstorming information. You just put down on paper anything that occurs to you, in no set order. It beats staring at an empty, blank page.
- You can use a mind map during presentations. It has the advantage of being on one piece of paper, and the key concepts are all there in front of you.

How to Make a Mind Map

1. Start by drawing (on page 118) an image in the center of the page to illustrate your main focus or idea.
2. Add a label to your image and write it in capital letters.
3. Underline words or put them in bubbles.
4. Stick to one word per line.
5. Similarly build your mind map, adding images and words throughout. Connect underlined words and bubbles as you go.
6. Color in images, if possible, as this enhances memory.
7. Allow your mind to wander as freely as possible. Too much conscious thinking about where things should go will simply slow down the process.

3. Structuring

When you have finished your mind map, add some structure to it. Choose the first topics that you put on your map and write them on a separate piece of paper. Then read the ideas that follow to develop your presentation notes.

Ideas for Structuring Your Talk

Be aware of the WIFT factor (see page 96–97). That means, "What's in it for them?" In other words, what any group will get out of listening to you. Your mind map may have been a general look at yourself, a hobby or a product you want to sell. Now concentrate on the areas that will really interest them.

A SAMPLE MIND MAP

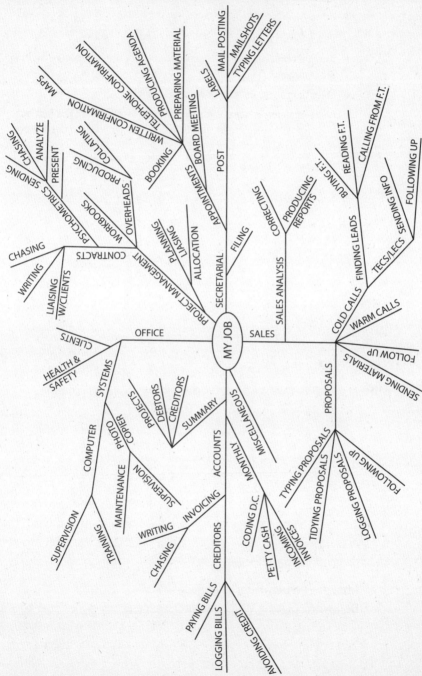

YOUR MIND MAP

Draw your own mind map

You might want to redo your 30-second commercial (see page 33–34) or try putting ideas down for a talk you are giving in the near future. Turning this page sideways will give you more space.

Wide of the Mark

Mark McCormack, a famous business guru (founder of IMG), was asked to speak at a conference in Northern Ireland. Throughout his talk, he mentioned the way large multinational companies ran their businesses. This would have been fine if it had not been a conference for small businesses. Part of his audience was bored, and the other half angry.

Look at primacy and recency: This means selecting the two most important points of your talk and placing them at the beginning and at the end. We remember so little from presentations—probably only two or so points, and these tend to be the first and the last things we hear.

Statistics and stories are very important. The left side of our brains likes facts and figures; the right, stories and anecdotes. And, as most people you will be talking to will have two parts of their brain functioning, you need to appeal to both sides.

Now, return to your mind map and start structuring. At each branch, you will want to have facts and stories. For those of you who find telling stories difficult, read on.

Stories

People enjoy hearing stories and anecdotes, especially if they think the story may have actually taken place, so make it sound personal, as though you had been there. Be very specific and give a few details. Do not be afraid to borrow stories and change the details. Poetic license is allowed!

WHY USE ANECDOTES IN YOUR PRESENTATION?

Anecdotes engage your listeners. They can imagine the whole scene clearly and can enter into your story with you.

Advantages of Telling a Personal Anecdote

- The audience hasn't heard it before.
- You won't forget it.
- You'll be perceived as more sincere.
- They enliven both you and the presentation.

What To Do When They Don't Laugh At Your Jokes

If you make a joke but get no response, simply move on to your next sentence and pretend it was never intended as a joke. Try not to look stunned.

How to Make Sure Your Jokes Do Not Fall Flat

First of all, make sure the humor is relevant to your presentation. Do not spring a joke on an audience out of the blue. Secondly, never tell a tasteless joke—they are totally inappropriate in a speaking situation.

Too Hot to Handle

At a Scottish Burns Supper, a male speaker had not realized that it was not an all-male event, and he had included a lot of sexist jokes. As he talked, the room got quieter and quieter, with absolutely no one laughing. The speaker became increasingly flustered, and broke out in a sweat. Humiliated, he finally sat down, never to be invited back.

How to Engage a Dead Crowd

With an unresponsive group, the best solution is to engage the audience in something active to get them going. Give them a question to discuss with you, the person sitting next to them, or within a small group—anything to shake off their passivity and get them involved.

4. Topping and Tailing

Follow these guidelines and you will have people sitting on the edges of their seats.

Blow Your Trumpet

- Begin with something that makes your audience sit up and take notice, such as an outstanding fact or compelling story.

The Contract

- Decide on what this particular group will gain from the presentation.
- Know how long it will take.
- Decide when you want to take questions.

Your Menu

- Know the structure of the presentation.
- Know how and why it relates to that particular group.
- Link it into further discussion.

B. *Tailing*

You should have a zinger conclusion ready, so if you are told that your time is up, you can seamlessly go to your closing statements as if you had meant to finish there right from the start.

The Attention-Getter
- Signal the end with a final astounding fact or compelling story.

The Summary
- Briefly re-state your main points: "Tell them what you've told them."
- Repeat why they are relevant to the audience.
- Explain what you want them to do.

The Final Statement
- Prepare and deliver a pithy final sentence of not more than seven or eight words, so that it is remembered.
- At the end, stop, smile, and be proud of yourself.

PUTTING IT ALL TOGETHER

Now look back to your mind map, and the topping and tailing reminders on pages 117–118. Fill in your responses below, and you'll have a thorough aid-memoir for your presentation.

Opening Line _____

The Contract _____

Relation to
audience _____

Agenda _____

Discussion
Main Point 1 _____

Connection
Main Point 2 _____

Connection
Main Point 3 _____

Connection
Main Point 4 _____

Conclusion
Summary _____

Last sentence _____

We're going to concentrate now on all the other aspects of pre-senting. You know how to put the presentation together, so we are free to focus on you.

"NIGHTMARE" QUESTIONNAIRE

This questionnaire gauges your attitude and appearance. For really honest answers, try giving this form to someone who attended your last presentation and ask them to fill it in with you.

When giving your last presentation, did you experience any of the following?

	Yes	No
1. When asked to present, did you see it as utter torment?	☐	☐
2. When you started speaking, did you feel and look awkward?	☐	☐
3. Did you gesture too much?	☐	☐
4. When tense, did you freeze like a statue?	☐	☐
5. Did you have the habit of looking at the ceiling or floor—anywhere except at the audience?	☐	☐
6. Did you fiddle with keys or change in your pocket when speaking?	☐	☐
7. When handling visuals, did you tend to drop them, or get them mixed up?	☐	☐
8. Did you look somber and serious when you presented?	☐	☐
9. When talking, did you often use long, complicated sentences?	☐	☐
10. Was your speech peppered with ums, ahs, and hesitations?	☐	☐
11. When speaking about your topic, did you lapse into jargon?	☐	☐

	Yes	No
12. Did you have a habit of using slang language?	☐	☐

13. When speaking, did you experience any of the following feelings?

	Yes	No		Yes	No
Breathlessness	☐	☐	Rapid heartbeat	☐	☐
Dry mouth	☐	☐	Tense throat	☐	☐
Blushing	☐	☐	Tense face	☐	☐
Sweating	☐	☐	Butterflies in stomach	☐	☐
Blotchy skin	☐	☐	Cold hands	☐	☐
Nausea	☐	☐	Feeling faint	☐	☐

	Yes	No
14. Did you feel a bit "past it" to be an effective presenter?	☐	☐
15. Did you feel too young to be taken seriously?	☐	☐
16. When speaking, did you feel conscious of your weight?	☐	☐
17. As a person, did you feel too ordinary to make an impact?	☐	☐
18. Was your presentation too dull and uninteresting?	☐	☐
19. Did you talk too fast?	☐	☐
20. Were you disorganized for that presentation?	☐	☐
21. Did you stand up feeling unprepared?	☐	☐
22. Would you be happy if you never had to give a presentation again?	☐	☐

BODY LANGUAGE FOR PRESENTATIONS

Facial Expression

You need a bright, lively, interested expression rather than a tense, serious face. Find something near the beginning of your talk to make you smile, either a story or a joke (see pages 119–121). Smiling is so captivating that it will get most audiences on your side instantly.

Eye Contact

Your eyes should be on the audience, not on your notes or your slides. Try to look at the audience as if you were talking to each individual.

The Eyes Have It

A Scottish chorus was visiting the USA. They were being conducted by Daniel Barenboim, who was exceedingly demanding. The chorus, although challenged, were determined to be the best they could be. After the concert was over, each member of the 200-strong group said, "Did you see the conductor looking at me?" Daniel Barenboim had the wonderful knack of making eye contact with everyone on the stage so that they all gave the performance of a lifetime.

Posture

A confident posture with a straight, although not rigid, back is preferable to an apologetic one. Taking a deep breath and easing back your shoulders helps you to make an impact.

Gestures

Gestures are good. They help to underline important points and add emphasis to your speech. So keep your hands out of your pockets and use open gestures.

Touch

At the end of a talk, it is great to make personal contact. A handshake is sufficient as a measure of appreciation to your listening public.

Distance

Make sure you are at a useful distance for easy scanning of your audience. Reorganize the room if you are uneasy about seeing every member of the group.

POLISHING THE VOICE

Being able to use your voice well improves the quality of your presentation. Projecting the voice, rather than shouting, means that not only will your audience be able to hear you better, but you will sound relaxed and in control. Getting the most out of your voice in terms of pitch, tone and pacing will add light and shade to your presentation, making what you say sound more interesting.

Breathing

Good breathing is essential for voice projection. You can use the exhalation of breath to carry your voice across the room. Good breathing is also important in phrasing, so that you don't end up gasping for air in the middle of a sentence.

How to Breathe

Take a deep breath. Now let it out slowly. Feel yourself use the diaphram to get that last burst of air out.

You may want to put your hand on your rib cage to feel it expanding and contracting.

Now take a deep breath. As you exhale, say the sound *oooh*.

Now repeat the exercise with the sound *aaah*.

"Placing" Your Words

The second important factor to consider when projecting your voice is where the words are placed in your mouth. If they are at the back of the throat, the breath has to push them much farther to make them carry. If they are already at the front of the mouth— just behind your teeth—then they're perfectly placed to be pushed directly across the room. Practice a few times saying a word the way you would normally say it, and then feel the word positioned immediately behind your teeth.

> ### How to "word-place"
>
> Take a deep breath and, as you exhale, again say the sound *oooh*.
>
> This sound should be placed behind your teeth, ready to be pushed out by the breath. Do this several times.
>
> Now repeat this exercise with the sound *aaah*.
>
> Take a deep breathe and say *n–tee–tah* as many times as you can as you exhale.
>
> Now do the same exercise using real words.
>
> Practice again using phrases and sentences.

Stressing Words

Often, people stress the wrong words in a sentence. If your message is to be clear, it's important that you use emphasis in the correct way.

> ### Test Your Emphasis
>
> Try saying, "*I think this is for you*" with the stress on a different word each time—and note the differences in meaning.

Tone

It's not what you say, but the way that you say it. You can say the same thing, but with another tone of voice, the message is very different. For example, you may sound angry, calm, cool, tender, sarcastic, nervous or friendly.

> ### Tone Test
>
> Think of as many ways as possible to say, "*You're really good at that.*"

Pitch

There is a danger, if you are at all nervous, to pitch your voice too high. Try to be aware of this, and practice your breathing and relaxation beforehand. If the words are "placed" in your mouth correctly, it is easier to maintain a pitch that both feels and sounds comfortable.

Timing and Pacing

Don't rush through your material, or your audience will think that you're in a hurry to leave. On the other hand, going too slowly can seem condescending—and boring!

Use pauses for effect in your presentation. When you've made an important point, pause. This lets your point sink in with the audience. Similarly, pause when you've asked a question. This allows the audience to think about the answer and have time to respond before you tell them.

Enunciation

We can get lazy in our speech and forget to enunciate consonants clearly. Try the following tongue-twisters.

TONGUE-TWISTERS

Say the following three times:

- I want some deep freeze peas please
- Six most delicious swiss rolls and a packet of mixed biscuits
- Seven dozen double damask dinner napkins
- She had inadvertently left her umbrella at the library
- You will find the text in the fifth verse of the twelfth chapter of the acts of the Acts of the Apostles
- There's no need to light a night light on a light night like tonight
- He chased a pup upon Upper Websters Street
- Try to think of six thin things and six thick things too
- He compiled innumerable lists of statistics

And try:

Red leather yellow leather	A knapsack strap
A threadbare bedspread	Hamlet's helmet
Twenty competing telegraphists	Romany Yeomanry
Six thistles	Peggy Babcock

Finish with the following from actor Danny Kaye (in *The Court Jester*, 1955):

The chalice from the palace has the pellet with the poison, but the vessel with the pestle has the brew that is true.

> As is our confidence, so is our capacity.
> *–William Hazlitt*

CASE HISTORY

Emily's Confidence Issue: Feeling she always has to look perfect

Emily, 23, is very pretty, has a secure job, and lives with her fiancé who loves her very much. She knows all of this but was behaving as if she had no confidence at all. It was essential to her that she always looked perfect. She felt her friends expected it, and that she must keep up with everybody's standards. In her view, if she did not do so, then her friends would judge her and form negative opinions of her. Consequently, she would never allow even her closest friends to see her without makeup. Any trip out of the house, however trivial, would be prepared for, in case she bumped into somebody she knew. Even a trip to the market involved her hair, nails and makeup being perfect. She would wear a smart suit and not dream of going in sweats. If she saw somebody when she was not prepared, she would run and hide. Once out, she was so self-conscious that she couldn't relax and feared something terrible would happen. She would think, "I will fall over." Consequently, she always tried to go out with her fiancé, and was very reliant upon him. This caused him to become frustrated with her, which lead to arguments. She also tried to avoid social situations when she could.

Emily also needed her home to be perfect, otherwise she was afraid that her friends would not like it. A lot of time and money was spent to make sure everything matched. She had to have the best.

Emily tried to be perfect in so many ways to try to cover the fact that she did not feel good enough and to give an appearance of confidence. It did not work, and her actions just made her feel even worse. Her motto was, "If I am not perfect, I feel low." She did not have the confidence to be her real self, as she felt she would be judged, and that people's opinion of her would be negative. She decided she was fed-up with pretending, and wanted to be confident enough to reveal the real Emily behind the mask of makeup and perfection.

Analyzing the Problem
Negative Thinking

Emily's Beliefs	Identifying the Inaccuracies
Friends expect perfection.	Wrong labels
People judge me and form negative opinions.	
I must keep up with everybody's standards.	Overgeneralizing
I'm afraid they won't like it.	Negative predictions
I'll fall over.	
I'm not good enough.	Poor self-esteem

Emily's Behavioral Patterns

Emily's Approach	Coping Strategies
Always looks perfect	Ineffective coping strategies
Very reliant upon fiancé	
Always wears makeup—never seen without it	
Excessive preparations for trips out of the house	
Has to have the best	
Runs and hides if someone sees her unprepared	Protective behavior—escape
Always has to go out with fiancé	Protective behavior—fears an audience
Avoids social situations when she can	

How We Helped Emily

- We asked Emily what she thought people who went to the market were thinking. Once she realized they were interested only in their shopping and not how she looked, she was able to see that her fears were unfounded.
- We encouraged her to attempt what she feared most—going out in public without her makeup.
- We challenged her to try new things.
- We helped her to recognize that her self-worth is not dependent on how she looks.
- We got her to visualize every step of a trip to to the market in her sweats with no makeup. Once she had imagined it, the reality was easy.

QUICK REMINDERS

√ Make new friends—use FORE on anything that moves (see pages 110–113).

√ Show people that you're interested in what they say and use open and probing questions (see pages 111–112).

√ Remember the Emotional Bank next time you have to talk to a very tedious person (see page 112).

√ It's normal to be anxious about presenting, but use the magic formula (see page 115) and it need never be a problem again.

√ Use effective body language (see pages 124–125). Look like you're enjoying yourself, rather than wishing you were hiding in the restroom.

√ Breath, otherwise you'll start hyperventilating and you won't be able to project your voice (see page 125).

√ Practice your tongue-twisters and let everyone hear what you are saying.

PROGRESS DIARY

What I've learned from this chapter	How I intend to put this into practice
1.	
2.	
3.	
4.	

DAY SEVEN

Staying Confident

Congratulations. You have completed the Confidence course in six days. So why a seventh?

When we read a book, complete a course, or return from any life-changing event, we are on a "high" for a number of days. Then, life inevitably intervenes. We return to the same people, the same jobs, and the same lives we left behind. Despite our good intentions to change, normality can overwhelm what we've learned. So we need to identify things that will help us to keep going when the going gets tough. Four areas come to mind:

1. Goals and goal-planning
2. Finding people to support and encourage you
3. Finding energizers
4. Reassessing strategies

1. Goals and Goal-Planning

Start by reviewing your life goals. You have already produced goals for this book (during Day One). Now you must broaden that view and look at the other areas of your life, such as your aspirations for your personal life: family, friends, children, hobbies, and your working life: skills, promotion, colleagues and leadership.

Confidence Tip

Focus on your long-term goals first, before you think about how you are going to get there using short-term ones. Choose one major goal and work through it in detail.

MY PERSONAL GOALS:

My Long-Term Goals | **What I want to achieve in** ☐ **years** | **Examples**

— — — — — — — — — — — Position?

— — — — — — — — — — — Income?

— — — — — — — — — — — Leisure?

— — — — — — — — — — — Family?

— — — — — — — — — — — Community?

— — — — — — — — — — — Possessions?

— — — — — — — — — — — Relationships?

My Medium-Term Goals | **What I want to achieve in** ☐ **years** | **Examples**

— — — — — — — — — — — Work activities?

— — — — — — — — — — — Position?

— — — — — — — — — — — Responsibility?

— — — — — — — — — — — Income?

— — — — — — — — — — — Leisure?

— — — — — — — — — — — Family?

— — — — — — — — — — — Relationships?

My Short-Term Goals | **What I want to achieve in** ☐ **months** | **Examples**

— — — — — — — — — — — Work activities?

— — — — — — — — — — — Responsibilities?

— — — — — — — — — — — Projects?

— — — — — — — — — — — Family?

— — — — — — — — — — — Leisure?

— — — — — — — — — — — Reward?

— — — — — — — — — — — Social life?

Choose one major long-term personal goal:
For example, you may want to work in France permanently.

What work goals do you need in order to achieve this?
Find out about the possibility of an internal transfer to the French office.

Medium-term goals to support the long-term goal:
You may go to France on a weekend to see the area in which you might be working.

What I need to do, short-term, to achieve my medium-term goals:
Start taking French language classes at a local college.

Therefore, I need to do the following work next week:

__ __ __ __ __ __ __ __ __ __ __ __ __ __ __ __ __ __ __ __

__ __ __ __ __ __ __ __ __ __ __ __ __ __ __ __ __ __ __ __

__ __ __ __ __ __ __ __ __ __ __ __ __ __ __ __ __ __ __ __

__ __ __ __ __ __ __ __ __ __ __ __ __ __ __ __ __ __ __ __

__ __ __ __ __ __ __ __ __ __ __ __ __ __ __ __ __ __ __ __

Discover Your Future Self in Five Minutes

Sports psychologist and motivator Pete Cohen teaches this effective visualization of your "future self" to help focus on your goals.

The problem is that when we have a problem, we tend to think about it a lot. And the more you think about something, the bigger it gets. You get what you focus on, which is a pity, because we all tend to be rather problem-focused. So, here's a way to get yourself moving in the right direction.

Find a quiet place where you can be alone for about five minutes. You need to feel comfortable, relaxed, and free from distractions.

1. Stand up with a couple of feet of space in front of you.

2. Close your eyes and see your front door in your mind. Make it a life-sized image, and imagine you're standing outside, turning the key, and pushing it open.

3. Imagine now, as your door opens in front of you, that you can see yourself through that door at some time in the future. You

are looking at yourself the way you would be if you didn't have your personal millstone to carry around any longer. Maybe you are looking taller, more confident, happier, calmer, slimmer, healthier, more relaxed. See yourself exactly as you want to be.

4. Notice the expression on your face, the look in your eyes and the clothes you're wearing. Make the picture so clear and bright that you could reach out and touch it. Make it vivid, colorful and brilliant. It doesn't matter if at first it's not as sharp as you would like. With daily practice, your image will become more real.

5. Now imagine the "future you" turning away from you, so that you are looking at your own back. Take a step forward and blend right into that back view of the way you'd like to be. Literally walk into your new body as if you were putting on a new skin.

6. As you do this, notice how you feel. Notice how at ease and comfortable you feel. Get a sense of the energy and power you will have as you open your eyes in the new you.

7. Repeat this exercise every day, and you will come closer and closer to becoming the "future you."

2. People To Support and Encourage You

People who lack confidence often surround themselves with people who sap their energy. Identify who they are in your life, and look for different people who will encourage and give you support.

- Who would you choose to help you feel better when you are down?

- Which friends, family members or colleagues will challenge you when you are not performing at full throttle?

- Who will coach you when you can't solve a problem?

- Which friends, family or colleagues will encourage you to keep motivated?

- Who, among those you know, inspires you to achieve?

- Who else can help you achieve your goals?

> The greatest pleasure in life is doing what people say you cannot do.
> *—Walter Bagehot*

3. Finding Energizers

- What could I do to make life more stimulating?

- What could I do to make work more fun?

- What could I do to make work less frustrating?

- What could I do to make work life less stressful?

- What could I do to make work a more creative place for me?

- What could I do to make life more challenging?

- What could I do to make life less routine?

- What could I do to grow as a person?

- What could I do to develop other people at work?

- What could I do to increase other people's happiness?

4. Reassessing Strategies

Deciding to Act—A Japanese Tale

There is a Japanese tale about a mythical bird that spent the daylight hours enjoying the sun and having a lazy time, while the other birds got on with the job of nest-building. When the sun went down and night came, the bird spent the night freezing, determining that tomorrow he would not hang around but would build a nest so that he did not have to suffer. However, when the sun rose, he did not act, but continued his acquired pattern of behavior and just enjoyed the sunshine.

Sound familiar? We all have habits that we find hard to break. However, unless we can see the benefit of changing, then we will not take action, let alone sustain it.

To assist you in your resolve, complete the following exercise:

- Think of what you want to change and then write it down on the top of a piece of paper.
- Draw a line down the middle of the page and, above column one, write "What if I do?" then, above column number two, write, "What if I don't?"
- Fill in the columns (spending a minimum of ten minutes doing so.)
- When you have filled in the columns, reflect on the consequences to you and others if you choose to act or not.
- If you do decide to act, write down and answer the following questions:

1. How? Think it through (how much, how do I, how do I start?).

2. When? Set yourself a time and place to begin. If possible, set for yourself three additional times for checking and review.

3. Who? Who are you going to get to support you? List two people who are going to help you in your determination. Their contribution can be as small as their just knowing, or as big as joining you in your quest.

If you decide not to act, then this exercise has helped you realize what you don't want.

A wide group of pensioners, surveyed some years ago, realized that their main regret was not taking more risks. Do not leave it too late to begin living the life you deserve.

Visualizing Success

During Day Four (pages 61–80), we explored our capacity for visualizing negative outcomes and disasters which, in hindsight, rarely materialize. To keep going, you must have a vision of the changed you in the the forefront of your mind. If not, you will forget what you want to become.

So, to practice visualization, you first need to relax.

- Sit on a comfortable seat or lie down on a bed or floor, supporting your head with a cushion.
- Take a deep breath and exhale slowly. Repeat.
- Tense and relax your arms and hands.
- Bring your shoulders toward your ears, then relax.
- Bring your chin to your chest, stretching the back of your neck, and relax.
- Tense every muscle in your face: forehead, eyes, nose, and clench your teeth.
- Take a deep breath and tense your stomach muscles as if preparing for a blow to that area, and relax.
- Tense your thigh muscles and relax them.
- Stretch the back of your legs, and turn your feet up toward your face. Relax.
- As you breath out, let your body become heavier and heavier, and increasingly relaxed.

When you are relaxed, imagine that you are the star in your own television soap opera. Visualize yourself as vividly as possible. Turn the brightness controls up on your imaginary television to achieve more definition and color in your vision.

First imagine the old you, with all that you would like to change, doing all the things you would be doing as the old you.

- What would you be saying?
- How would you be acting?
- What would you be worrying about?

Visualize these things for just a minute.

Now, change channels with your remote control. You are now looking at the new you—how you want to be. What would you now be doing—who would you be with; what would you be wearing; how would you be looking; how would you be feeling? Place some adjectives beside this image of the new you—for example, happy, relaxed, successful, confident.

Add whatever adjectives you desire to your visions.

See this television image enlarge itself and move off toward the horizon. Visualize the new you going toward the future, and tell yourself, "This is how I will be." Place a realistic date beside this vision and believe that it will happen. Gradually come back to "real" time and repeat this exercise every night before going to sleep. Success will be yours.

Emily and Maria's Vision of Success

In *Confidence Lab*, Emily and Maria used visualization with great success. Emily, when relaxed, visualized walking through a supermarket in sweats without any makeup—her major hang-up. She imagined meeting friends and neighbors without feeling anxious or that they were judging her as unattractive. She felt confident and assertive.

At the end of this exercise, she felt liberated from years of thinking that she had to look perfect. Being herself was just fine. People had told her this, of course, but visualization provided her with the personal experience.

With Maria, we used her presentation to the police as her TV soap opera. She visualized preparing her presentation, arriving at the venue, entering the room, scanning the audience, making the speech, and then being congratulated by those in attendance. Instead of being apologetic and girly as she was prone to be, she felt assertive, witty, confident—a truly successful performer.

This visualization technique, coupled with the Power Minute (see page 44) from Day Three just before presentation and mind-mapping (pages 115–118) from Day Six helped her make a great impact when she later made her actual presentation.

CASE HISTORY

> Trust yourself: every heart vibrates to that iron string.
> –Ralph Waldo Emerson

Jo's Confidence Issue: To build her confidence and stay motivated

Jo, 43, has spent most of her life being dominated—first by her parents, and then by her ex-husband. She had had a lifetime of being told off and made to feel she was useless. Eventually, she came to believe it. She had no confidence in her own abilities and felt she had to depend on others. But at 43, she suddenly found that she had to depend on herself. With no husband, home or job, she had to rebuild her life herself. She realized she would need confidence to change the habits of a lifetime. She came to *Confidence Lab* with a full agenda, determined to make it work. She wanted to change. "I have never been more ready," she said, and eagerly spent the week developing practical skills and learning more about herself. Gradually, she began to realize that, "The only person holding me back is me... I can do anything if I believe in myself." She left feeling liberated—like a new woman.

Then, however, she had to return to her isolated, empty house. She was alone again, back in the real world, and she needed to build the confidence she had gained in order to keep things going by herself.

Initially, she lived on an adrenaline high, with lots of energy, and enthusiastically started a lot of new activities. Then, as was inevitable, she began to encounter her old real-life problems, and she felt down. This was an important turning point for Jo. This was the time at which she was most vulnerable and at risk of going back into her shell. She could utilize her new skills in solving these problems or fall back on her old, ineffective coping strategies. Jo decided that she had gained so much from *Confidence Lab* that she owed it to herself to keep things going, thinking, "If I go back now, I will lose so much.'

Jo motivated herself to do this by focusing on, and fully acknowledging, the number of positive gains she had made, and by being realistic about the negatives in her life. The new high was not sustainable: "I was waiting for [the high] to come down... now I am on a level which is sustainable... I prefer ups—shame about the downs—but that's life. I am just going to have to put ups in my life." She looked only to herself to put the ups in. "I know it's up to me... it's my life. I am the only one who can make me happy and, if anybody else does, it's an extra bonus."

She accepted that all her old problems were still there, and, as *they* were not going to change, she had to. "My position hasn't altered, but my perception of it has," she says. Changing her perspective allowed her to take a new approach to problems that she had previously felt were insurmountable. She used the skills she had learned to help her. For example, a long-standing problem of hers was feeling lonely. Rather than accepting this, Jo drew on the social skills she had learned and made a real effort to meet people. She started new activities, initiated conversations with people she didn't know, and kept in touch with them. "I've started the gym, salsa classes... afterward, I ask, Anybody for a drink? This is something I'd never have done before. My phone bill is much higher than it used to be." She no longer screens her calls. Now she answers the phone and returns messages, too.

If nothing is going on, she will organize social events herself—another first for her. "I thought that, as there was nothing happening on Saturday night, I'd make it happen. Before, I would have stayed in and watched TV."

There were problems Jo realized that she could not fix, but she changed her attitude toward these, too. "I don't let things upset me as much anymore... I feel calmer—and not so aggressive toward people."

There are times when she still gets low, and she is learning the importance of turning to her friends for their support and help.

As well as support, Jo also has a special friend who is very honest and acts as a benchmark for her. This allows her to continue to monitor her progress and provides an additional person to make sure she does not slip back into her old ways.

Jo's positive steps forward

Positive thoughts

Jo's Beliefs	Identifying the Inaccuracies
Change the habits of a lifetime	Accepting the need to change is a crucial first step
Determined to make it work	The desire to change—more than just realizing the need to change, she must be prepared to do so
Never been more ready	
Only person holding myself back is me—I can do anything if I believe I can	Self-belief—realizing you can bring about new changes in your life yourself
Operating on a level which is sustainable—not feeling shame about the downs—that's life, there are problems I can't fix	Being realistic—having normal expectations of what change will bring; there will always be negatives or setbacks; put them in perspective and don't exaggerate.
I'm going to have to put ups in my life	Self-realization; putting change within your control; learning to draw on your own strength and abilities
It's up to me—it's my life	
I am the only one who can make me happy	Changing labels—looking at things differently is sometimes the only thing you can change
Nothing happening on Saturday night, so I will make it happen	
My position has not altered, my perceptions of it have	
I don't let things upset me as much anymore	
Rather than accepting	Re-evaluation: look at your life.

Jo's Behavioral Patterns

Jo's Approach	Coping Strategies
She came to *Confidence Lab* with a full agenda	Broaden horizons—seek and take advantage of positive opportunities to help bring about change
Utilize new skills	Changing ineffective coping strategies—identify what you do, and replace it with more constructive/protective behavior
Focus on the positive gains	Self-motivation—identify positive reasons to continue and maintain your change; make a list and refer to it at difficult times
She used the skills she had learned to help her	Application of new skills—don't just learn them, use them
Learning the importance of turning to her friends	Identifying significant others, a valuable source of support and motivation
Continue to monitor her progress	Self-monitoring: during the early days especially, it is easy to slip back into old habits

QUICK REMINDERS

√ Review your goals constantly—long term, medium term, and short term.

√ Be discerning about which friends you choose to support you. Select the most positive who have your best interests at heart.

√ Pursue energizers for the rest of your life.

√ Every day, visualize success.

PROGRESS DIARY	
What I've learned from this chapter	**How I intend to put this into practice**
1.	
2.	
3.	
4.	

Appendix

The Authors: *Contacts and Publications*

Ros Taylor

Plus Consulting
Office 2
St. Saviour's Wharf
23 Mill Street
London SE1 2BE

Publications:
Fast Track to the Top (Kogan Page, 2002)

Recordings:
Visualization and Problem-Solving
Deep Relaxation and Quick Relaxation
Think Plus

website: www.plusconsulting.co.uk
e-mail: ros@plusconsulting.co.uk

Roy Leighton

Lamda Business Performance
Tower House
226 Cromwell Road
London SW5 0SR

Corporate and Educational Training
T: 020 7373 3446

Guest Therapists

Here are details of the guest therapists who appeared on *Confidence Lab* and their publications.

Eileen Mulligan

Eileen Mulligan is one of Britain's most successful and high-profile coaches. After building up a million-pound company in the beauty industry and winning Cosmopolitan Entrepreneur of the Year, she became a business consultant trouble-shooter, and life coach. Her clients include members of parliament, media personalities, industry leaders and top executives.

Books:
Life Coaching—Change Your Life in Seven Days (Piatku)

Pete Cohen

Pete Cohen works as a sports psychologist and personal trainer and is well known for his work with Lighten Up, a revolutionary slimming program. He uses techniques for people with low self-image, phobias, or lack of motivation to empower them to build confidence in themselves.

Books
Slimming with Pete Pete Cohen & Judith Verity (Crown House Publishing, 1998)
Feeling Good for No Good Reason Pete Cohen & Judith Verity (Essentials, an imprint of How To Books, 1999)
Doing It with Pete Pete Cohen & Judith Verity (Crown House Publishing, 2001)

Audio Cassettes
Slimming with Pete a step-by-step guide to the Lighten Up method.

Stewart Pearce

Formerly trained as an actor teacher, Stewart has worked as a voice coach and presentation consultant for over twenty years. He has been consulted by many famous actors and leading public figures such as Minne Driver, Ross Kemp, Julia Ormond, Vanessa Redgrave and Anita Roddick.

Stewart is currently Master of Voice at Shakespeare's Globe Theatre.

Allan & Barbara Pease

Allan Pease FRSA is the world's foremost expert on body language. His acclaimed book *Body Language* sold more than four million copies in 32 languages. He works with his wife Barbara who as CEO of Pease Training International, produces videos, training courses and seminars for businesses and governments.

Videos
Body Language Series
Silent Signals
How to Make Appointments by Telephone

Audio Cassette Albums
Why Men Don't Listen and Women Can't Read Maps
The Body Language Workshop
The "Hot Button" Selling Workshop
The Four Personality Styles Workshop
How to Make Appointments by Telephone
How to Develop a Powerful Memory
Questions Are the Answers: How to Get to "Yes" in Network Marketing

Books
Why Men Don't Listen and Women Can't Read Maps
Body Language
Talk Language
Memory Language
Write Language
Questions Are the Answers: How to Get to "Yes" in Network Marketing

Pease Training International
12 Umberslade Hall,
Tamworth-In-Arden
West Midlands B94 5DF

Tel: 01564 741 888
Fax: 01564 741 800
www.peasetraining.com
email: peasetraining@compuserve.com

Kerry Ribchester

Kerry Ribchester is a world-class dance teacher, specialising in Cuban dance. She has worked extensively with the C.N.E.A.R.T. academy in Havana, and also teaches salsa courses in Spain Miami and Puerto Rico.

What makes her work special is her unique understanding of the body in motion, gained through a decade of training in body-mind centering. She is also a qualified Hellerwork (bodywork) practitioner.

Video
Salsa from within Cuba. How to Dance Salsa from Beginner to Advanced Levels.

For details of the salsa and dance courses in Cuba, Miami, USA and Puerto Rico call Dance Holidays UK. Tel: 01206 577000

Accreditations

Day One
Confidence Checklist — Ros Taylor, Plus Consulting Ltd

Day Two
Journey into the Past — Ros Taylor, Plus Consulting Ltd
Backpack Exercise — Roy Leighton
Casing the Joint — Ros Taylor, Plus Consulting Ltd
PAC Questionnaire — Eric Berne, adapted by Ros Taylor

Day 3
30 Second Commercial — Ros Taylor, Plus Consulting Ltd
Body Language Figures — Ros Taylor, Plus Consulting Ltd
The Power Minute — Ros Taylor, Plus Consulting Ltd
The Five Minute Nerve Buster — Roy Leighton
My Hero — Roy Leighton
Own Your Own Space — Roy Leighton
Career Drivers — D. Francis
Train Exercise — Ros Taylor, Plus Consulting Ltd

Day 4

Labeling Exercise	Ros Taylor, Plus Consulting Ltd
Sentence Completion Exercise	Ros Taylor, Plus Consulting Ltd
Reality, Outcome and Useful Thinking	Ros Taylor, Plus Consulting Ltd

Day 5

Emotional Language Exercise	Ros Taylor, Plus Consulting Ltd
Stroking Patterns Exercise	Ros Taylor, Plus Consulting Ltd
The Four-Step Process	Ros Taylor, Plus Consulting Ltd
Psycho-Geometrics	Sue Dellinger
The Anger Exercise	Ros Taylor, Plus Consulting Ltd
Animal Exercise	Ros Taylor, Plus Consulting Ltd

Day 6

FORE	Ros Taylor, Plus Consulting Ltd
The Emotional Bank	Laurence Clarke
What Makes a Good Presenter	Ros Taylor, Plus Consulting Ltd
Nightmare Questionaire	Ros Taylor, Plus Consulting Ltd

Day 7

A Japanese Tale	Roy Leighton
Discover Your Future Self	Pete Cohen
People to Support and Encourage You	Ros Taylor, Plus Consulting Ltd
Finding Energizers	Ros Taylor, Plus Consulting Ltd
Visualizing Success	Ros Taylor, Plus Consulting Ltd

Index